30

RESPECT
FOR LIFE

RESPECT FOR LIFE

REPORT OF A CONFERENCE AT
HARPER'S FERRY, WEST VIRGINIA
ON
The Traditional Upbringing
of American Indian Children

EDITED BY
Sylvester M. Morey and Olivia L. Gilliam

Illustrations by Warren P. Jennerjahn

MYRIN INSTITUTE BOOKS
New York

CONTENTS

ILLUSTRATIONS

United States Department of the Interior
BUREAU OF INDIAN AFFAIRS
WASHINGTON, D.C. 20242

IN REPLY REFER TO:

To make a complete person is the first responsibility of education. If a child is to learn, the stage must first be set so he will want to learn. The various tribal cultures recognized and practiced this tenet. It is certainly a principle that should be a part of today's educational process, especially in a society as complex as ours. This conference of American Indians on traditional Indian education, along with the prior conference, is of tremendous help in making the philosophy available to people concerned with the education of all children.

I sincerely believe the spirit of cooperation exhibited in this conference will continue to grow and result in greater efforts to find a way to combine intellectual and intuitive teaching methods to help transform the education of both modern Indians and modern white men to reach a common goal -- a better society.

Morris Thompson
Commissioner of Indian Affairs

March 12, 1974

The Myrin Institute is grateful for the help and cooperation of the Honorable Robert L. Bennett, Commissioner of the Bureau of Indian Affairs in 1968; the Honorable Louis R. Bruce, Commissioner in 1972, and the Honorable Morris Thompson, Commissioner in 1974.

INDIAN INTUITION:
AN INTRODUCTORY COMMENT

In recent years there has been an about-face in the approach to teaching young Indians. Until very recent times, children on reservations were frequently shipped off at a very tender age to government-financed boarding schools where they were given white man's names and taught the language and customs of the white man. Severe punishments were often handed out to children who continued to speak their native tongue or to observe the traditional rituals of their tribe.

For a long time, Indian parents have protested against rearing their young as though they were white children. Colonial records of Pennsylvania for the year 1744 give testimony to this fact. In June and July of that year, commissioners of colonial Pennsylvania, Maryland and Virginia held a long conference with representatives of the Five Nations of the Iroquois. Near the end of the meeting, George Thomas, Lieutenant Governor of the Province of Pennsylvania, invited the Indians to send several boys to Virginia, "where," he said, "we have a fine house for them to live in, and a man on purpose to teach the children of you, our Friends, the Religion, Language and Customs of the white people — and we promise you they shall have the same care taken of them, and be instructed in the same manner as our own children."*

Canassatego, spokesman for the Iroquois, declined the invitation with thanks and indicated that the Indians loved their children too well to send them this distance from home and, besides, did not desire to give their children this learning.

Now, nearly two and a half centuries after the 1744 meeting, our country is becoming increasingly aware of the fact that all is not well with the way education has developed in white America, not only for young Indians but also for all our children regardless of race and color. We have acute problems with so many young people who do not find joy in life, who get involved with drugs and alcohol, who drop out of school or take part in senseless crimes.

The Myrin Institute for Adult Education felt it was time to examine the traditional Indian views of education — a subject skipped over in 1744 and little considered since then.

In 1972, the Institute invited leading Indians from widely separated tribes to come to a meeting in Harper's Ferry, West Virginia, and there to spend a week discussing the traditional Indian's views of the upbringing and education of children from birth through adolescence.

Obviously, it is impossible for Indians or anyone else to turn the clock back so as to live again in the way people lived here in colonial times. Much, however, can be learned by understanding how Indians formerly approached life and how they felt children should be guided from the cradle upwards.

The Institute did not undertake this meeting in the blind hope that it might be lucky enough to stumble on solutions to today's problems. The meeting at Harper's Ferry grew organically, rather, out of a previous meeting with a group of Indian elders in Denver in 1968, also sponsored by the Myrin Institute. The 1968 meeting gave ample evidence of the fact that there is still much intuitive wisdom in the red man's traditional concepts that can be applied to the white man's contemporary problems.

---

*The Colonial Records of Pennsylvania, 1735-1745, Vol. IV, pp. 729-735. (June 17 — July 4, 1744).

What prompted these meetings

It may seem strange that an organization such as the Myrin Institute, which has little contact with Indian affairs, should suddenly start holding conferences with Indians, to seek their views on controversial matters. There are no anthropologists connected with the Institute nor others who consider themselves Indian "experts." The Institute's interest in Indians came about in a rather personal way in which the writer was involved. Therefore, the following explanation seems in order.

Some fifteen years ago, I learned that the Austrian philosopher, educator and seer, Rudolph Steiner (1865-1925), had stated that much of the success of the white man in America was due to lingering effects of the intuitive wisdom of the American Indian. The thought struck me, as I had not been aware that white men had made use of Indian wisdom to any great degree or, for that matter, that Indians had much intuitive wisdom. I resolved to look into the matter and to my amazement found that, indeed, many ideas we have made use of in our daily lives were originally Indian. In 1961 I gave a lecture on the subject for the Myrin Institute at the Waldorf School of Adelphi University. The lecture was published by the Institute, and many readers seem to have found interest in it.

The average white American still thinks of Indians as inferior people, with no fixed abode and no organized political or social systems. But the Jesuits who lived with the eastern Indians back in the seventeenth century spoke with admiration of the Great Council of the Iroquois. For example, the Jesuit Lafitau compared it with the Roman Senate in the early and rude age of the Republic, and affirms that it loses nothing by the comparison.*

Benjamin Franklin copied the concept of the League of the Iroquois in his plan of union for the Colonies, as presented in Albany in 1754. "Neither an anthropologist nor a romancer, Franklin looked upon the Indian always with the humane curiosity and natural respect which he felt for any people whose way of life was different from his own. He admired the Iroquois

---

*F. Parkman, *The Jesuits in North America in the 17th Century* (Boston, Little Brown and Company, 1970), p. LVIII.

Confederation, and plainly had it in mind in his earliest discussions of the need of union among the colonies. 'It would be a strange thing,' he wrote, 'if six nations of ignorant savages should be capable of forming a scheme for such a union, and be able to execute it in such a manner as that it has subsisted ages and appears indissoluble; and yet that a like union should be impracticable for ten or a dozen English colonies, to whom it is more necessary and must be more advantageous, and who cannot be supposed to want an equal understanding of their interest.' "*

The late Felix Cohen, noted attorney and scholar, wrote this about Indians in general: "It is out of the rich Indian democratic tradition that the distinctive political ideas of American life emerged."** Then he went on to point out that it was the Indian who first had suffrage for women as well as men. It was the Indian who first developed the idea of a state within a state (the League of the Iroquois and other Indian confederations) that we copied when we created the United States out of our thirteen Colonies. It was the Indian who treated chiefs as servants of their people instead of masters. And I can add that it was the Indian who showed Americans how to be generous — a quality that has become truly American and even now distinguishes Americans among the peoples of the world. Another fact little realized is the extent to which team sports as they have developed in America appear to have been an Indian idea. Stephen F. de Borhegyi, Director of the Milwaukee Museum, made this point some years ago in an article in *Natural History Magazine.*** It seems rather evident from what I have read that team sports were unknown in Europe before the 16th century — and the idea for them came back to Europe from our native Americans, along with the idea and material for a rubber ball.

In the course of making other interesting observations about Indians, Mr. Cohen throws light on the origin of the most popular phrase in our language today. He says, "Even the sole

---

*C. van Doren, *Benjamin Franklin* (New York, Viking Press, 1957), p. 209.
**F. Cohen, *The Legal Conscience* (New Haven, Yale University Press, 1960), p. 317.
***"America's Ball Game," by Stephan F. de Borhegyi, *Natural History Magazine*, January, 1960.

American contribution to the vocabulary of democratic government turns out to be a word borrowed from an Indian language. When Andrew Jackson popularized a word that his Choctaw neighbors always used in their councils to signify agreement with another speaker, the aristocrats he threw out of office, always grasping at a chance to ridicule backwoods illiteracy, accused him of abbreviating and misspelling 'All Correct.' But 'O.K.' (or 'okeh,' in Choctaw) does not mean 'All Correct;' it means that we have reached a point where a practical agreement is possible, however far from perfection it may lie. And that is central in the American idea of government."*

Perhaps the Indian's greatest intuitive contribution to American life came through his reverence for nature, his close connection with animals and vegetable life, with the weather and the landscape of this country as a whole. The Indian's intimate knowledge of nature was an immense help to the early settlers and could be of still greater help to America now, if we would really understand and properly apply it, in bringing our environment back into balance.

How the Denver meeting started

In 1967 I decided that an attempt should be made to broaden public awareness of the fact that there had been such a thing as intuitive wisdom among the Indians and at the same time find out if the Indian elders alive in our day still possess this wisdom. This project was discussed with the Honorable Robert L. Bennett, then Commissioner of the Bureau of Indian Affairs in Washington, D.C.

At the suggestion of Dr. Franz E. Winkler, President of the Myrin Institute, I told Commissioner Bennett that the Institute would be glad to sponsor a meeting of Indian elders, if he would select the Indians. Our plan was to hold a week-long meeting and to give the Indians, who would come from different tribes, the opportunity to tell us of their philosophy of life, their legends, as well as their tribal views of what should be

*Cohen, *op.cit.*, p. 317.

done to improve modern life and find solutions to contemporary problems.

Mr. Bennett was very much interested in the idea. He picked the men. We met in Denver for five days and had what was probably the frankest discussion on philosophical and spiritual matters ever held between Indians and whites in modern times. The Indians were:

Alfred Bowman, Navajo, New Mexico
Ben Black Elk, Oglala Sioux, South Dakota
David Kindle, Navajo, New Mexico
Guy Quetone, Kiowa, Oklahoma
Alex Saluskin, Yakima, Washington
Chief Joshua Wetsit, Assiniboine, Montana

Others who sat in for some sessions were:

Sydney Carney, Seneca
Forrest Gerard, Blackfoot
Francis McKinley, Ute
Will Rogers, Jr., Cherokee
Clarence Wesley, San Carlos Apache

Allen C. Quetone, son of Guy Quetone, was Chairman of the conference and proved very able in keeping the meetings moving. All the Indians were helpful and interested. After the second day an atmosphere of confidence had been established that permitted all to speak without restraint. At the end of the conference, Dr. Winkler and I, who represented the Institute, felt we had made warm friends with the Indians and that we were cordially joined with them in a common cause — that of trying to make people aware of the fact that, even today, Indians possess a certain way of looking at human life and the life of nature that our country needs. Their intuitive wisdom is something different from the intellectual knowledge of white America. If the country could combine the two, we felt, many of our social and educational problems would be overcome.

As Dr. Winkler said in summing up our meeting in Denver: "The United States today is clearly at a crossroads. In their brief history, the American people have built the strongest, richest and most generous country in the world. Yet the use of drugs, racial strife, crime and violence, are reaching epidemic proportions. In other words, our civilization is one-sided; blessed by an abundance of intellectual abilities and technological skills, it is sadly lacking in an intuitive grasp of qualitative values such as the pursuit of true happiness through love of man and nature, through philosophical contemplation, and through religious experience. The Indian people, on the other hand, are endowed with intuitive faculties that may restore to American culture the inner strength it so badly needs in this crucial era.

"History itself demands a basic reconciliation between the two cultures, for the reason that a conquering civilization has seldom, if ever, flourished without receiving strength from the forces already existent in the conquered country. In America these forces have been weakened by our suppression and neglect of the Indian, but in my opinion they are still alive and full of promise.

"The path toward a living together of the red and white civilizations for mutual benefit must start with recognition of their differences rather than with any attempt to reshape Indians in the image of white Americans. While it is the task of our government to provide Indian leaders with every possible opportunity to rebuild their own culture, it is up to the Indians themselves to bring what is so great in their heritage into a form appropriate to 20th century conditions. Since the wheel of history cannot be turned back, a restoration of Indian culture will have to be thoroughly modern, without, however, accepting the blatant errors and pseudo-scientific materialism of modern America and Europe.

"Do not nurture in your children a sense of bitterness and revengefulness against white people, for those who have committed the real crimes against Indians have long since gone from the earth."

Robert W. Fenwick, who at the time wrote up the meeting in the *Denver Post*, headed his story, "Indians Hold Pow Wow on White Man's Ills" and his lead paragraph read, "In an extraordinary change in traditional field positions, the American Indian was asked to Denver last week to ride to the rescue of the beleaguered white man."

A report of the meeting, which included verbatim statements made by the Indians as well as comments and explanations given by Dr. Winkler, was published by the Institute in a book entitled, *Can the Red Man Help the White Man?** This book has since been twice reprinted.

The meeting at Harper's Ferry

After the first attempt to focus attention on the intuitive wisdom of the American Indian, in order to bring about greater understanding and mutual help between red man and white, the Myrin Institute felt it should sponsor no further meetings unless they were requested by the Indians themselves. In 1971 such requests were received, and one of those who asked for another meeting was the Honorable Robert L. Bennett, who had done so much to help set up the first meeting but by then had left the Bureau of Indian Affairs and was teaching law at the University of New Mexico.

The topic of the new meeting, as indicated before, was to be education. Following Dr. Winkler's death, at the beginning of 1972, John F. Gardner had succeeded him as President of the Myrin Institute, and as Mr. Gardner is an educator and was to play an important role in the meeting, the reason for the selection of this topic was obvious.

The Honorable Louis R. Bruce, then Commissioner of the Bureau of Indian Affairs, was consulted, and he offered his good services in helping Allen Quetone select the Indians and make other arrangements for the second conference. Mr. Quetone had done such a fine job chairing the Denver meeting that we were most anxious to have him fill the same role in the second meeting. It was decided to ask younger Indians this time. It was again suggested that they come from widely separated tribes and that the number should remain at six or eight. If the group were to be much larger, there would be no chance for the members to come to know each other well

---

Can the Red Man Help the White Man? ed. Sylvester M. Morey (New York, The Myrin Institute, 1970).

enough in a week's time to develop the confidence necessary for an intimate discussion.

The training quarters for National Park Rangers at Harper's Ferry, West Virginia, was our meeting place, and we all roomed in the large dormitory of an adjacent building. There was a very good hotel a few blocks distant where we ate three meals a day together. This further contact proved to be an important factor, as the informal "breaks" gave us the opportunity to fortify our mutual respect and understanding.

All discussions with the Indians were held in traditional Indian style: that is, each person who spoke had the floor for as long as he had something to say; no one interrupted him, and everyone paid attention. Furthermore, the Indians continued to have something of interest to say, day after day. As the week progressed and we came to know each other better, there was much joking and good humor but there was also a deeper interest in the real purpose of the conference — to tell white people the true Indian view of life as expressed by members of the various tribes represented at this conference.

In the beginning, we ran into a little procedural problem in our formal morning and afternoon meetings. We had broken down the subject of child rearing into different age periods, something like the chapter headings in this book. But the Indians did not wish to be limited in this way. They said that they could not talk to us about how they would handle a baby or a child at any age unlesss we first understood their overall view of life. It was very fortunate that we had our informal evening discussions in the dormitory and at meals. Through hours of interesting talk, not recorded, we learned what the Indians meant by viewing life as a whole. Out of this outlook came their key word: "respect" — respect for the child, for the mother, for the home, the clan, for all people; respect for animals and plants, for the weather, for the sun, the moon, the stars, for Mother Earth; and above all, respect for the great spiritual force that stands behind all and makes life possible and worthwhile.

When the Indians were convinced that we understood and agreed with them in the need for this respect, our discussions proceeded smoothly and to good purpose. Then they dealt with the child at various ages. We have transcribed their conversations here as they were given but not necessarily in the sequence in which they were given. The conversations taken all together are what make up this book, *Respect for Life*.

SYLVESTER M. MOREY

The Indians who took part at Harper's Ferry were:

Jimmy Begay, Navajo, Arizona
Ernest Benedict, St. Regis Mohawk, Ontario, Canada
Max Hanley, Sr., Navajo, Arizona
Henry Old Coyote, Crow, Montana
Stella Old Coyote, Crow, Montana
Allen C. Quetone, Kiowa, Oklahoma (Chairman)
Victor Sarracino, Laguna Pueblo, New Mexico
Arthur Sutton, Arapaho, Oklahoma*

The Honorable Louis R. Bruce, Mohawk-Sioux, Commissioner of the Bureau of Indian Affairs, officiated at the opening of the meeting. Also attending as secretaries were Mrs. Dene Curtis, Cherokee, and Miss Barbara Wilson, Navajo. Mrs. Tommie Leahy, Cherokee, represented the Bureau of Indian Affairs Public Relations Office.

Representing the Myrin Institute were:

Sylvester M. Morey, Chairman
John F. Gardner, President
Marion G.H. Gilliam, Vice President
David A. Barten, Assistant to Mr. Gardner
Olivia L. Gilliam, Executive Secretary*

*Cf. Appendix for biographical information on the conference participants.

xxii

Left to right: Arthur Sutton, Allen Quetone, Max Hanley, The Honorable Louis R. R. Bruce, John F. Gardner, Stella Old Coyote, Jimmy Begay, Henry Old Coyote, Ernest Benedict, Victor Sarracino, Sylvester M. Morey

1
THE SPIRITUAL HERITAGE
OF THE AMERICAN INDIAN

ALLEN QUETONE: It has been proposed that our discussions cover the traditional methods used to teach and instil values in Indian children from the time of their birth to early adolescence. We know that the philosophies, myths and legends used in traditional Indian education contain great spiritual truths and determine the way the Indian people look at their being here on earth. I think many of us in the Indian world still believe in a greater power that controls our lives and the things that we do; we believe there is a definite relationship between the human being and nature. Many of the tribal priests and medicine men had visions that had some relationship with the spirit world but which have no rational explanation. Both my father and grandfather saw certain visions and heard certain stories that would not be believed by young Indians today who have not been exposed to the same spiritual realities as our older Indian people.

Most of today's young Indians are just like non-Indians. I mean, if they don't see it, they don't believe it. It has to be touched, it has to be seen. Our forefathers were not that way. There were certain things they believed in; and because of their faith, these things often happened. These happenings would never be doubted by my grandfather, for example. Knowing the honesty and integrity of that man, I would be the last person to doubt his experience of miracle-like phenomena. Both of my grandfathers were boys while the Kiowas were still roaming the Plains. One died when he was 101 years old; the other lived to be 99 years old. These two gentlemen's lives extended from the tribal-traditional era of the Indians to the modern twentieth century, thereby giving me and others an opportunity to be exposed to the natural-spiritual philosophy that is our heritage as Indians and is a substantial source of our possession of God's gift to the Indians — intuitive perception.

By exploring our heritage at this conference, we will try to discover some of the attitudes and methods that were used by Indians to teach their young. While we recognize the historical value of this information, our interest is not as historians but as human beings who have come to realize that our Indian forbears displayed great wisdom in preparing the individual for life. We would like to benefit from the wisdom of our past, and hopefully we can do so.

There have been experts, sociologists and anthropologists, who have spent their lives studying all aspects of the Indian way of life. They have used the appropriate technical language to describe our behavior, our mores, our beliefs. Whatever our philosophies and our religion, they have classified them and written them into scientific papers. You can go to any library in the country and you will find this material on the American Indian. But what impact, what influence has all this had? And scientific study of the Indian has been going on for at least a hundred years! If anything, it has complicated our status as Indians. We have become drawing-room subjects of historic Americana — or even worse, museum pieces.

Here at this conference we are not trying to please anybody. We are just going to say it as it is: as we are, as we were taught, as we see the world about us, and have seen it from the time of our fathers and our grandfathers before us. It's not as if we were going to sit here and have somebody take a telescope to look at us and get inside our minds.

The reason I am saying this is that while I was at Oklahoma University, there were many anthropologists who had projects going. They would sit down with their informants and get the type of information they wanted in order to fill in the blank spaces they had. They would get just so far in their writing, then they would need to round it out; so they would keep asking questions until a particular Indian said what fitted in to make the study complete. But our approach will be somewhat different.

The area we hope to cover is one that is hard to define. It is the deeper concepts that hold good for all men. We, as Indian people, feel strongly that our way is a good way. People thrive under it because it somehow gives the human being those things that make him happy, make him satisfied with life. This is what we are hoping to get at.

SYLVESTER MOREY: When we know each other a little better, I think you will find that we are in complete accord with what you have just said, because we are not trying to claim that things must be so and so, to fit a preconceived scheme. We are asking the Indians to tell us what they believe; then we hope, by using what we are told, to help improve education in this country.

ARTHUR SUTTON: Sometime ago there was an anthropologist who came to my home town, and he invited me to speak with him. He asked me all kinds of questions and I just studied him myself. I said, "Oh, oh, this fellow's trying to use me. That won't do. I'm going to cut him off in a minute."

He said, "What is it?"

"Whatever you're writing down," I said, "Don't publish it; don't sell it."

He said, "Why?"

"Those are my own experiences," I said. "If you want to understand more about our culture, best thing for you to do is to come and live with us and stay with us and find out for yourself. Then you'll have a better understanding, better background; you'll know where we stand."

He looked at me sort of funny and said, "What do you mean?"

I said, "I know you. You'll go back and make a name for yourself, and all you have done was ask questions. How can you tell? I may tell you a lie. But now I'm telling you the truth. A person who really wants to understand Indians must come directly to where the Indian lives, in order to see *how* he lives, *how* he gets along. That's the best I can tell you."

HENRY OLD COYOTE: I believe I can understand the gentleman from Arapaho's* view, because I know that Indians have certain reservations about what they want to relate to others. At one time when the Christians came into our territories, they suppressed our beliefs and practices. They termed us pagans, heretics, and what have you, and they discouraged us from practicing our ceremonies. I remember that the Bureau of Indian Affairs even got into the act, and if a Crow Indian went so far as to have a sweat lodge, he got 30 days in jail. The Indians haven't forgotten this; it's the reason they're reluctant to relate their experiences to people they don't know. They aren't certain whether these people are sincere or whether they are out for their own personal gain. We have too many two-bit writers in the country. You can't say anthing without having someone pick up the information and build on it so that you no longer recognize it after it's in print.

That's what the Indians are leary about today, because they haven't forgotten the fact that their practices were suppressed, that the dominant society tried to make white people out of them. One time an Indian said, "They're trying to make a white man out of me. But that's not the color of my skin. I may learn the white ways, but I'll still be an Indian." So that's why a lot of Indians had to go underground to practice some of their customs.

Today the opposite is true. Now we have Indian experts popping up all over the country. Everybody's trying to tell us that this is the correct way, the authentic way of presenting our customs and beliefs. But the real traditional Indian is staying in the background, trying to see what goes on. I consider myself a traditional Indian. There are three types: traditional, transitional, and non-practicing Indians. And according to the advice I've been getting, I keep my ears open and my mouth shut.

MAX HANLEY: May I interrupt a little bit? I listen over here and over there and I would like to tell you something. When I first entered school it was 1916. That year, I ran off with some boys; they were going to have a ceremonial, what

---
*Arthur Sutton

they call the Blessing Way. Of course, I'm just the first time at school. I don't know anything about the white man's way. So I went along in the wagon. I took off with them, about six or seven of them. I stayed over there all night. But the principal checked on the boys and the boys were gone. The next day he found out where we were. So we told him, "We had a little ceremony over one of the students who had a bad dream to clear up; otherwise, something was going to happen to this boy." The principal asked us, "Do you believe in medicine man?" Everyone says, "Yes." "Yes." "Yes." I had just come up from the brush or hogan and didn't know better, so I said, "Yes," too. All of us were put in jail for what we believe. We stayed in jail for 15 days.

Now in those days, BIA was trying to destroy our culture. We couldn't talk our own language, Navajo. Every time the principal or one of the employees heard us talking Navajo, he punished us. We were not to talk in our own language, or sing, or go to any kind of ceremonial. You had to forget all this. It was very compulsory.

As time went on, somehow they'd found out — through education, through philosophy — that it's not good for the Indians if the schools take away whatever they believe. They have to stay with it. So this is what our brothers, the white people, now say: "This is not good for them. You're taking their own religion away from them." The other side is turned around. They've found out what's good for us!

Today they claim there is a gap. They want to fill this gap through Indian education. Yes, we can fill up all these gaps and make them smooth. So let's work together, whites and Indians. Here's a white horse and there's a brown horse. Let's get together; let's pull together, and we will make a good education for these younger people in the next ten or twenty years.

ALLEN QUETONE: I am sure that most Indians are beginning to know that this is not strictly the white man's world. Most of my life I have heard about white man's education, white man's this, white man's that. This is the way the older Indians were conditioned, and it resulted in their withdrawal from the dominant society's way of doing things. But today I think we are more aware of the fact that it is our world, too.

None of us pretends to be an expert in education, although most of the Indians at this conference are in some way involved in Indian education, and Mr. Gardner is an educator in his own right. But each of the Indians here has been exposed to both the traditional Indian and the twentieth century white man's way of doing things. Each of us, therefore, has a practical and real relation to the subject we plan to discuss.

JOHN GARDNER: As you have indicated, Allen, the traditional Indian way of education rested on intuitive understanding. The Indian, at least the grandfather Indian, once found the hand of God everywhere. The white man's way — characteristic not of every white man but of our modern, industrial white civilization — rests on an intellectual outlook that finds the hand of God nowhere. It is becoming clearer every day that insofar as young people, whether they are white or Indian, are brought up in schools where facts are but facts and natural laws are merely abstract formulas, and God is nowhere, the white man will degenerate; and the Indian, too, will inevitably lose the spirituality that once gave him his health of body and mind.

I am in education, and I watch young people in schools that are predominantly white; I see that many of the youth are going to pieces morally, and that we older people are wrecking the beauty and health of this American continent, to say nothing of the earth as a whole, mankind's home in cosmic space. All of this disintegration and destruction is the result of a certain attitude, and it is with the hope of changing this attitude that we at the Myrin Institute are so interested in the Indian point of view. Unless something changes in the white man's habitual attitude, he will wreck himself, he will wreck this planet, and he will carry the red man down with him.

In what way should we turn to the Indians for help? Let's suppose that people try to bring back the ceremonies, legends and traditional beliefs of the Indian and try to give them credence and honor so that they influence the prevailing culture. What value would this have if the Indian himself has lost, as many young Indians seem to have done, his original understanding of the spiritual reality behind these traditions?

As soon as you lose personal experience of the spiritual facts and events that stand behind ceremonies and sacred traditions, these ceremonies and traditions become nothing more than superstition. Nobody will give his heart to something he regards as superstition.

We are interested in establishing the fact that there are two ways of knowing and that both are legitimate. One is the more brainy, intellectual way and the other is the more heartfelt, intuitive way. The traditional Indian has stood for the latter and the white man, at present, stands for the former. Both must be brought together in a new form of education. If we whites could learn to regard the world with the profound understanding that was typical of the Indians of earlier times, we could change the current destructiveness of our society. This is one of the things we are interested in exploring at this conference; it is of first importance to us.

ALLEN QUETONE: So the value of this conference is that we Indians have an opportunity here to look at ourselves and examine our heritage. Instead of being studied by anthropologists and having our traditions interpreted by people who have no real understanding of them — and I personally don't like to be studied — we can express our own experiences and thoughts concerning what we were taught. We should look at ourselves as Indian people and bring to the fore those things that we still hold dear, that we live by. Arthur, you reflect exactly what your grandmother taught you, right or wrong. Okay, it's this whatever you are that we would like you to share with us in these sessions. We hope that you will impart the wisdom, the experience, the knowledge you have gained as a leader of your tribe and thus bring us to a better understanding of the Indian way of life.

VICTOR SARRACINO: I cannot go into many details of the religion of the various fraternities, for example, because even as an Indian I cannot attend some of the traditional ceremonies unless I'm initiated. But I'm willing to share those ideas that I can with you.

I truly believe that there are certain things in the Indian way of life that are good for everybody — even for those who may not profess any belief — because there are a lot of things

that relate to nature. A lot of our Indian people can qualify to
be ecologists because this is what they do at home. They believe
in nature, in purification, in prayers, and it's that belief that
keeps them going. Even during planting time, they seem to
relate to anything that grows out of the ground, and to the
good air, to the sunshine and clouds and all these things. I don't
think anybody can dispute this. It's really their way of life.

I have a mother who has been a midwife all her life, ever
since she was a young girl. She talks about a lot of things she
used in the way of herbs and medicines, and some doctors
nowadays agree that these are the right things to use and do. I,
for one, also grew up with my grandfather. I guess my dad
passed away when I was about four or five years old. I can't
even vaguely recall ever talking to him, but I was told that I
followed him everywhere he went. Soon after, he passed away,
and I lived with my grandfather. He lived to be 104 years old.
So that's who I learned from. He said he was sent off to
Carlisle, where he studied philosophy, so he was quite a
philosopher and storyteller. Sometimes I believed him and
sometimes I didn't; but the older I get, the more I am
convinced all his stories were true.

In my tribe, the Laguna Pueblos, there are still quite a
number of people who know that their way of life is based on
religion, their own religion. In fact, they even say it's more than
a religion, because you live it 24 hours a day, not just at certain
hours. But as the others have said, many of these people from
various denominations did come in and little by little took over
and converted our people to their own churches. Today some of
our people do believe in other denominational groups and
forego their own religion for fear that you cannot serve two
masters.

ALLEN QUETONE: Back home in Oklahoma, the
missionaries made such headway among our people that about
half of the tribes are Christian and half are traditionalists. The
result of this split was dissension and disunity, which was
reflected in all traditional and political meetings of the tribe. I
grew up during this period of my tribe's adjustment. I heard
both sides, and feelings were very strong. So when I became
active in tribal politics and won a seat on the council, I went to

both groups. My father is a Christian, and fortunately or unfortunately this is the way I was reared. There is one thing that rises above our differences today. I mean, we can't go back, however nice it would be. This country of ours, America, permits us to believe however we choose under the religious guarantee in the Bill of Rights. If you want to be a traditionalist, that's your right; if I want to be a Christian, that's my right.

Personally, I'm of the belief that there is only one Higher Being and it's the same one that we all pray to and look to for the type of sustenance man has always needed. I just don't believe there is that much difference between religions. Each represents a different road, a different method, of approaching God or the Great Spirit.

VICTOR SARRACINO: I guess we Indians are afraid that some of our young people are beginning to think like the other society, but it's wrong to have this attitude because our young people are thinking in their own way.

JOHN GARDNER: Young Indians know there is more to life than they are being told in the course of their ordinary schooling in the white man's world. They are beginning to look, and non-Indian young people are looking as well. I have heard that many Indians, even the grandparents, have forgotten the inner ways; it is important that we find them again for the sake of Indians and whites alike. I believe we can help each other.

HENRY OLD COYOTE: Allen, mind if I say something? In just about every school I have visited that is teaching Indian courses — colleges, high schools, and probably some elementary schools — the staff are trying to categorize the Indian culture. But among my people, the Crow Indians, you can't categorize the social or religious life of an Indian the way the white man does, because everything is interwoven; it's all one ball of wax.

I was just sitting, listening and thinking about the agenda you have here. How am I going to separate Indian beliefs and tell about one way over here and another way over there, like name giving, childbirth and all that? Because everything is connected, and our belief enters into every aspect of our life. At least, that's the way it is with my tribe.

JOHN GARDNER: We take for granted what Henry just

said. Religion, surely, is not some set of beliefs. It either goes through everything and touches everything with a sacred element, or it touches nothing. It's one or the other. We share your view; so any time you talk that kind of language, we understand you perfectly. If religion doesn't touch everything, we wonder if it touches anything.

I would like to make a remark about what was said earlier concerning the Christian missionaries. As I see it, what was objectionable about some of the missionaries was not their Christianity, but the way they taught and practiced it. For a long time, those who represented Christianity have tended to exclude other religions. Dogmatic missionaries have said, "This is pagan; that is heresy; this is no good; give that up." I don't believe this attitude is true of real Christianity, but this is the way many Christians have thought and still think today.

Christianity has paid a terrific penalty for this narrow-mindedness. The penalty is the following: after this dogmatic, mean-spirited idea of Christianity had pushed out everybody else's religious experience except its own, there was only one thing left to happen. Something still narrower, still more limited, came and pushed the Christian doctrine out: namely, the technical scientific point of view. This kind of scientific view throws out Christianity along with all the other religions and beliefs.

Trying to bring back the religious life of the Indian is the difficulty we face. We really can't succeed unless we get right down to the root of the matter and ask, "Is the Indian experience true, or is it not true?" One cannot build real devotion, enthusiasm, and discipline on anything less than real truth. Neither the narrow dogmatism of pseudo-Christianity nor the still narrower materialism of pseudo-science believes or admits or has any way to conceive that the sacred lore of the Indian is true.

This brings us to the special nature of this conference. We come to meet you with an attitude fundamentally different from that of most missionaries or educators or anthropologists. We believe that the Indian religious experience of life — in its original, pure form — is true, is based on objective spiritual truth. And we don't think it is in conflict with what is original and pure in Christianity, either.

VICTOR SARRACINO: My grandfather used to say: There's going to be a day when the Indians and the Europeans are going to meet, and they're going to have to iron something out to be in harmony.

SYLVESTER MOREY: Your grandfather must have been a great man. What he said is absolutely true.

When we met with Indian elders in Denver in 1968, the point was made that the Indian and the white man have never understood one another, but it's the Indian who is going to understand the white man before the white man understands the Indian. This is so because the Indian can think with his whole heart, whereas the white man thinks with his head, and thinking only with the head really doesn't help one to understand the other person. We are not experts, but fellow men. We want to hear what you have to say.

ALLEN QUETONE: With all of this in mind, let's turn our attention to the traditional upbringing of children in the Indian world. From the time of conception and pregnancy, we Indians regarded the child in a manner that is fundamentally different from the viewpoint we encounter today in the white man's world. Let us therefore unfold the story of the Indian child's life as it was lived in the traditional way, beginning with the period just prior to birth. Vic, would you like to begin?

2
CHILDBIRTH

VICTOR SARRACINO: During pregnancy, a young woman is taught always to have good thoughts and be joyful, regardless of what happens. Even if there is a death in the family during this time, she is taught to believe that death can be the happiest moment for that individual, because he or she is going on to the land of paradise. So everyone tries to keep the young lady happy. When she and her family eat at table, they speak about all things that are good and will bring joy to the child. This is the way we philosophize, and the women really take it in.

Sometimes there are superstitious thoughts while the young lady goes about her chores. For example, if a pregnant woman should see a snake trail when she is walking or going after water at the cistern, she is advised not to cross over it until she has brushed it off with her right foot. If she crosses over it without following this advice, she is told that her child will be born with teeth. So a woman looks out for little things like this. She knows they have something to do with taking proper care of herself during pregnancy, such as making her walk slowly while she is still carrying the child in her womb.

During the last two months before the child is born, a woman is not allowed to do sewing of any kind, either with a bone or needles. They believe it will have as bad an effect on the child as if they talked about sad things or thought bad thoughts. Since these bad thoughts go into the system of the child, it is very important that the mother think positively with happy thoughts.

During these last two months, the young ladies drink a special kind of medicine that is made from boiled herbs. When laboring begins, there are usually four or five women who assist; they continue to give this medicine which they claim kills certain pain. Just prior to childbirth, they take an Indian belt that has been blessed and tie it around the mother's waist where the pregnancy is. Instead of taking pain killers, the woman hangs onto this belt when she is in labor; she keeps pushing on it and eventually the birth comes about.

Immediately after birth they turn the child upside down and hit him over the back so that he can take his first breath. After that, they bathe him in the yucca weed twice during the first day. Of course, they pray a lot as they do this. Just before the day is over, they paint the baby with white clay; they put it all over the body from head to toe and keep it on for four days. The clay is supposed to prevent the child from getting too much hair on his body and to cleanse all the substances that covered him prior to birth. On top of this, they put ashes on the forehead and all over the head so that the child will grow as the days go on. It also reminds them that someday the child will turn back to dust. I guess all of this was done to me. I don't recall, but that's what I was told.

Soon after birth, the navel cord is cut from the child. The spot where it is cut sometimes gives pain as if it continued to look for the "lost" link with the mother. In order to get that little thing to quiet down, they have a certain kind of rock which they heat and put on the spot that is paining. That thing usually shrinks to nothing and if it doesn't, they claim it will show up several months or several years later as a tumor.

The mother lies resting for four days after giving birth and is not supposed even to get up. She keeps the same belt that she used during labor tied tightly around her stomach so that when she takes it off, her stomach won't sag. At the same time she takes a hot medicine called "glug" medicine for four days and then for another four months. It is supposed to delay the menstrual periods. It is a recovery thing; the women really believe in it and it's been proven that it does help them physically.

The mother feeds the child from her breast, and all the things she has learned, and all her good thoughts, begin to go into the system of the baby. This is our belief. All my brothers and sisters were breast-fed except for one brother. He was reared on something called "Eagle Brand," and to this day people say, "Well, he hasn't left that bottle yet. He's still at it!" He won't let go of that bottle, meaning that he's drinking, and he's always being teased. I guess he's the only one out of my family who drinks alcoholic beverages. But teasing aside, many of our people think that it is bad for children not to be breast-fed.

During the four days the mother is resting, the child is being cleansed and washed with this white clay. On the fourth day, the boy child is given a bow and arrow, plus a rattle and a pair of moccasins. A girl is given a pottery doll or a little kachina doll.* On the morning of the fifth day, the medicine man comes and extends two eagle feathers toward the mother and child and raises them from the floor. He prays that there will be many spiritual things in the child and that he will grow strong. Then he takes them out through the doorway to meet the rising sun. At that time, many prayers are offered, using corn pollen and the charm stones that go with it. And in that early morning the baby is given a name, which he carries from that day until he dies. They pick the name based on something they see that early morning that has a relation to the child's clan. For example, if it happened to be the Water Clan, as in my case, and they saw a watersnake coming, they would probably name that kid "Watersnake." Whatever the name is, it has to be connected with the clan.

When the baby is brought back into the house, he is put in a crib. This crib is provided by the uncle, because they claim that in future years the uncle will have a lot of responsibility for this child. In other words, if anything unpleasant needs to be said, it will be up to the uncle, not the mother or father. So the

---

*A small, painted wooden doll representing one of a host of mythical spirit ancestors. Ed.

VICTOR SARRACINO —
Laguna Pueblo

uncle goes out into the forest and looks for a tree that has been struck by lightning. If wood has been struck by lightning, my people believe that the crib which is made from it will help to cure sickness.

The way we see it, this crib is a crib of turquoise and the hood over it is the rainbow. There is a song for this cradle, which the mother sings. It goes something like this: "Go to sleep, my baby. You are lying on this beautiful cape of turquoise and the rainbow is over your head. So sleep well."
And if the child cries, the mother sings, "Why do you cry, my baby? You are sleeping on this turquoise and I bring you these beautiful flowers. So go back to sleep."

Following the birth of the child there should be no man and wife relationship until the ninth month. There should be no sexual relation for the simple reason that if the mother's internal organs are disturbed, plus her emotions, she could become anemic and look pale and weak. By the same token, the child would begin to feel neglected; he would feel neglected as the mother nurses him and would begin to lose the true sense of love and affection. It would make the child grouchy and unpleasant and cause him to grow up to be a little brat. This is one of the things they teach our young women and young men. I would like to add that in our pueblo there has never been any birth control practice.

MAX HANLEY: This is the first time I hear how the Pueblos develop a child, and it is very close to what the Navajos do. In the Navajo way, quite a few things happen. First, where does the child come from; how does he start? Some people over here work together, of course, to have the child start. Then a month or two before the birth of the child, a medicine man is called to hold a prayer meeting one night. The night after the prayer meeting, they have a sing over the mother of the child so that the child will be born without difficulty or defect.

Both the mother and father have to be very careful until the child is born. Before then, they are not supposed to carve wood, or do what we call "fork" weaving, for fear the baby will be born with six "forks" or fingers. They are not supposed to burn deer hide, or horsè hide or any kind of hide to make a rope or whip. If they do, everything will be tied up and the mother will have a very hard time in labor.

And like Vic says, suppose they're walking along somewhere and run into a snake trail. They are not supposed to step over it; they have to drag their feet across it instead. Or when they're walking out there in the field, looking for a horse or herding sheep, maybe a coyote runs across their path. This is another dangerous thing. They're not supposed to go where the coyote passes. They have to turn around and go home and get their corn pollen. Our old traditional people usually carry corn pollen in their pockets. When this coyote crosses their path, they put corn pollen there and say, "Whatever you wish for me will never happen." They put corn pollen across the track and go on so that everything will be okay.

While the mother is in labor, they take a rope made out of the yucca plant and rabbit skin, which they braid together so that it's soft. There may be a little hole somewhere, either in a tree or hogan, where they attach the rope and knot it so that the mother can hold onto it. Another person, usually a man who is strong, sits behind her. He puts his arms around her stomach and tries to push down — easy, easy, easy, till the baby comes out. As soon as the baby is born, they cut his navel cord and wash him in cold water. Then they wrap him up. A long time ago they used to get the yucca, which they cut really small and wound around turkey or dove feathers to make a little crib. That was the first thing they wrapped the child with in the old days.

In the hogan or shed where the baby is born, there is usually a fire in the middle and a door on the east side. They put the baby on the west side, just a few feet from the fire so that his head will be kept warm. They keep him there for about four days. Then they get a cedar tree — not an old one, but a young cedar — cut the boughs off and cut out the inside: the part you call the sap, that is nice and white and juicy and tastes good. They split this inside and cut it small and put it in warm water, not to boil but to sit for maybe a couple of hours. Then they put in a pinch of corn pollen and give the child a little bit — maybe half a teaspoon. Sometimes it makes the child vomit. During birth he may have swallowed something, so he vomits it out.

After about four days, the mother feeds the baby at her breast. At least, that's the way it was in the old days. Nowadays they don't breast-feed anymore; they use the bottle. A lot of the traditional people complain about it. "You don't use your breast anymore; you use the bottle and cow's milk. That's why the younger generation no longer listen to their parents, why they run away from home and do what they please. In the past when children fed at their mother's breast, they listened to their parents."

HENRY OLD COYOTE: When a woman is expecting, it is up to a relative to alert the male and female members of the father's clan. The father's clan are the people we respect. They are the ones who more or less control our lives, because they are the ones who advise us; they provide spiritual guidance and they are also our public relations people. A certain amount of advice comes from the parents, as well as the grandparents and the mother's brothers, but spiritual guidance comes from the clan uncles and aunts. So the clan uncles and aunts merit respect; in this instance, they are the ones who express good thoughts for the one who is expecting.

When the baby is on his way, the mother and father may call on a clan uncle or aunt to make wishes for the child. Sometimes they make wishes and direct them to the moon, whom they address as 'Grandmother.' Tell that to a non-Indian and its nonsense, but the moon is used to keep track of the expectancy period — we speak of so many moons. The clan aunts give advice to the expectant mother and encourage her to move about. By moving about herself, she is giving the child-to-be some movement; she is helping his blood to circulate.

There are times when the clan uncles and aunts can foretell whether the child is going to be a boy or girl. Don't ask me how they do it, but through the sincerity of their belief they sometimes have a vision and see a baby boy or girl, or a grown-up boy or girl. Even when no one is expecting and they are simply fasting and making peace with themselves, they may have a vision or hear a name which they know is for a child who is to be born at a future time.

You might call it superstition, but before a child is born, the mother refrains from looking at anything deformed, for fear it may come out in the child. She also refrains from making fun of anyone. If a mother were to ridicule or laugh at a poor person, the child might be born poor. I was born poor; my wife married me when I was poor, and I'm still poor, I guess. At least, that's what my wife tells her sisters!

If the father goes out while his wife is expecting, he doesn't go hunting. He doesn't want to kill anything, especially the female of a species, since she may be expecting. If he kills an unborn animal, he himself may end up with a stillborn child. But if he has to go hunting, he goes through a special ritual beforehand. When he starts out, he takes something that belongs to his wife and shoots that object first. Then he goes and kills the animal. Since he has already shot something that belongs to the expectant mother, it's all right to go ahead and kill an animal. The men of some clans do it differently; they leave their gun on the ground and let their wife step over it. By stepping over it, they're breaking the taboo, just like breaking the trail of a snake. Our people refer to guns or any weapon as a sharp instrument. If you display a sharp instrument in the presence of an expectant mother, the harm these sharp instruments cause may be transmitted to the offspring. Therefore they want to break this taboo.

And so the child is born. Among my people, the number four is sacred. It represents the cardinal points, the seasons, the races of mankind. So it is on the fourth day after a birth that four clan uncles, or three clan uncles and one clan aunt, depending on the sex of the child, are invited to visit the newborn. They are the ones to select the child's name. Each person will suggest four names; the names are based either on the deeds and accomplishments of that person or on some vision he or she may have had while fasting. There may be a warrior among the four, or a good housekeeper, or a woman who tans hides; or some good person may have gone out fasting and had a vision of an animal or bird. Each of the four will suggest four names, and it is up to the parents or close relatives to make the final choice. As soon as the name is selected, they take the baby, make incense out of bear root* and pass it over the child four times. The fourth time they pronounce his name, and the child is henceforth known by that name.

What a person is doing when he gives a name is identifying the child to the Supreme Being. When he passes the incense back and forth, he is making his wish known to that Man up there. "If ever I mention this name, I mean this person here." While he gives the child his name, he paints him with red clay. This, too, is a mark of identification. "I'll put this on, so that You up there can recognize him."

If one of our people is traveling with a small child, it is our custom to call the child's name and tell it, "We are taking this child. So whoever you are, come along with us. There are some good days ahead." By doing this, we hope to coax the child's spirit to accompany his body to wherever he is going. If the spirit stays behind, if you don't call it, the child will get restless; he will sense something is missing and get cranky. But if you call the name, the child's spirit will go along with you and the child will be content.

ERNEST BENEDICT: As I listen to the traditions of the people from the western portions of this country, I feel culturally deprived. As you know, the Iroquois have been under a lot of pressure from the European world for several hundred years and we have not had enough people to withstand this pressure. The best way of safeguarding our most cherished traditions, we thought, was to appear to accept the new ways without doing so in fact. This may have been a dishonest thing, but it was natural, and the only means we could devise of preserving what was dear to us. But in the process, many of our traditions were lost or absorbed and we were forced to change our ways. I wish I could recount the traditions of my people in their pure form. Instead, I must describe what they have become and what I know them as — a somewhat blurred and often faint shadow of their original strength.

Bear root is the root of a plant belonging to the carrot family (*Leptotaenia Multifida*). Ed.

To begin at the beginning, they told me that my birth was on the reservation in a rather small house, and that my grandmother — my mother's mother — was there to attend. A midwife was also called to assist. Of course, even this has changed, because almost no babies are born at home nowadays.

Quite often the baby is given a name that belongs to the clan. In my case, I was given the name of my grandmother's uncle, that is, my great great-uncle. And so these names are passed on. They are taken from the old Iroquois language and quite often are rather hard to translate. My name refers to a betting game and means the bets or possessions that are put up as a stake, like the pot in a poker game. So they refer to me as 'Pile of Goods.'

As the children grow up, they often give each other play names. Most of these become the name by which that person is known until he is really old. Someone may be called 'The Preacher,' another, 'Raccoon.' There are people I know only by their nickname and not by their English recorded name or the Indian name that is given them at birth. Actually, our Indian names have been pretty well downgraded. It's only recently that they are beginning to come back because of a revival of tribal awareness and identity among my people.

VICTOR SARRACINO: I would like to add one word before we go on. When a child is born, a kind of rededication of the entire family takes place. We become child-centered again. We say, "Here is one who is newly born and who calls for our full attention." If it is a boy, the grandmother will begin to take sides with it and jokingly say to her husband, "Old Man, I guess you're going to have to move aside. I've just found a new lover, a new mate." Or she might say, "Well, we have just planted the flower, and it's going to bloom; in fact, it's already blooming. Now the way to keep this flower in bloom is to water it with love and care." This is what she tells the mother and what the mother is taught to do. The grandparents usually have fun arguing over the little child. If it's a boy, the grandfather will say, "Well, I'm a better hunter than that little kid." And the grandmother will answer, "No, you're not!" And so it goes. The entire family has the understanding that it must water the flower of birth, meaning the child, with love and care. This is what we believe and try to live by, even now.

3

DISCIPLINE
OF THE CRADLE BOARD

MAX HANLEY: When the child is almost a month old, the father or uncle goes out into the woods to get a cedar tree or piñon tree or ponderosa pine. They cut two separate boards about three feet long from the trunk of this tree, then shave them until they are really thin. These two flat boards are tied together in the middle to make what we call the cradle board. Also in the middle, a little hole is made for ventilation that we call the Permanent Spring (Drawing 1). It's like a little spring against the mountain where there is some green grass and maybe trees. So the baby lies down on the cradle and the air comes through this little hole and makes him feel cool and nice.

Over the baby's head are four staves that represent the rainbow (Drawing 2). The string tied at the bottom of the rainbow staves represents the sun's rays. The face cover represents the dawn and is brought over the rainbow rib, then dropped down to the feet. In the old days, my people used buckskin for the cover, but later on after the white man came, they used cloth — a white cloth because the face cover represents the white of early morning coming up. White is what the Indian sees at dawn. At noon, the sky turns blue; in the evening, it turns yellow; at night it turns black. Black, white, blue and yellow — all these four colors originated under the world. That's why you always see black, white, blue and yellow

A curved opening between the two boards:
the Permanent Spring

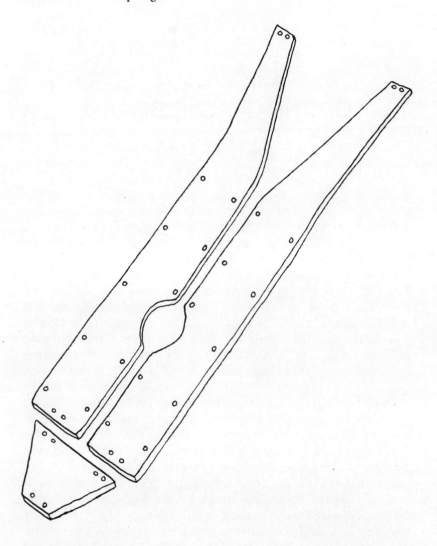

1. NAVAJO Cradle Board

on an Indian arrow right under the feathers. Haven't you ever noticed?

There are some holes along the outer edge of the cradle board through which you lace a long strip, maybe of buckskin. This buckskin strip represents lightning and is used to hold down the face cover. At the bottom of the cradle board is a foot rest or what we call a shield. When it is tied so that it stands upright, the baby rests his feet against it; it is also a protection, because if an arrow or spear were to hit this shield, it would fly right off.

On each side of the two tips of the cradle board are two holes from which doeskin ribbons hang. These ribbons represent the stormy rain; they represent the hair, too — long hair. The old traditional Indians say you are not supposed to cut your hair. When you cut your hair, there'll be no more rain. What happens nowadays? Where we come from, there's no rain. All these girls cut their hair today. It's too short; they cut the rain off. Anyway, all of these things give you some idea of what the cradle board is like and what each part means and makes us think of when the baby is lying there.

VICTOR SARRACINO: The Indian people believe there is a definite connection between human life and nature. And so all things that are of nature are used in rearing the child. This goes for the cradle as well, which is made from nature and represents the natural world. The material used to make the cradle is pine that has been struck by lightning. We have to go into the mountains to look for such a tree, and once it has been found, we cut three pieces from it and plane them down. The center piece is what the child lies on. One side piece is for the blue corn; the other is for the white corn. So we have three pine boards that are bound together with deerskin (Drawing 3).

There are four bands or guards that we color and place at the head of the crib. They start at the top edge of one of the side boards and go in an arc shape to the top edge of the other side board. These four bands represent the rainbow and we actually think the child will visualize the beautiful rainbow as he's being spoken to. They also represent the sacred four — the four seasons of the year, the four directions, the fourth epoch of my people. My people claim that it is the fourth evolutionary

24

A.   Permanent Spring opening
B.   Four wooden staves − Rainbow
C.   Face covering − Dawn
D.   Foot rest
E.   Lacing loops − Lightning
F.   Lacing − Sun's ray
G.   Deerskin ribbons − Rain
H.   Jingle toy

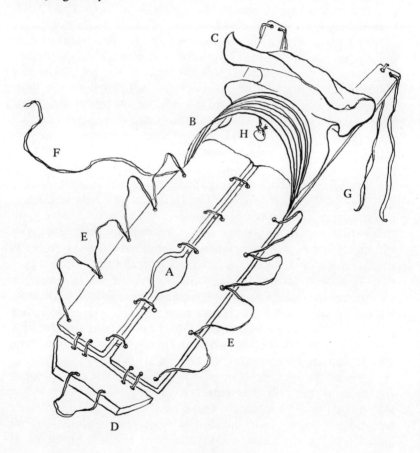

2. NAVAJO Cradle Board

period of their existence and that there will be three more before the end of the world. There have been three already in the past, and we are now in the fourth one.

The bottom of the crib is then covered with deerhide, which could be white or yellow or red. The baby is laid on this and is covered with more deerskin. Four loops are put on each side of the crib — almost anything the Indian does in our Pueblo area is in fours — and a strap is attached and laced over the deerskin coverlet so that the child is tied in. This laced strap represents lightning, and the skin that covers the crib represents the clouds. And as I said before, the whole cradle represents turquoise; it is a bed of turquoise for the child.

During the day when the mother is doing her chores and has to go outside, she will take two ears of corn that have been blessed and lay them on each side of the child. One is blue and the other is white. The Indians seem to be religious 24 hours a day; they keep in mind that these two ears of corn will be guarding the child. The mother also ties a little bag of dried deerskin at the foot of the crib which has been blessed in a ceremony. It contains charms like turquoise and agate as well as an ear of blue corn and white corn. As the mother goes out, she talks to the child; she talks to the corn and to the little charm stones and asks them to protect the child while she is outside. In the event the child wakes up, she depends on these things to put him back to sleep. The reason we don't put a piece of support on the back of the cradle is to keep it flexible so that the corn can roll next to the child if the mother rocks him, or ties him in a special manner, or picks him up. The corn sort of falls in with the child; it makes him feel secure and puts him back to sleep. Also, if you rub the corn on the side of the cradle, it makes a sound like a rattle. So if the child wakes up while the mother is outside or begins to kick, the corn makes a noise and puts him right back to sleep.

ERNEST BENEDICT: The cradle board used to be very important among the Iroquois and the use of it survived until approximately the time of my own birth. It was a half and half situation then; my family didn't have a cradle board, but most of my school friends were put on cradle boards, and most of them were breast-fed. Since then, of course, things have

26

A. Four bands representing rainbow
B. Four loops for lacing
C. White corn
D. Blue corn
E. Deerskin bag containing charms and corn
F. Lacing strap representing lightning
G. Foot rest

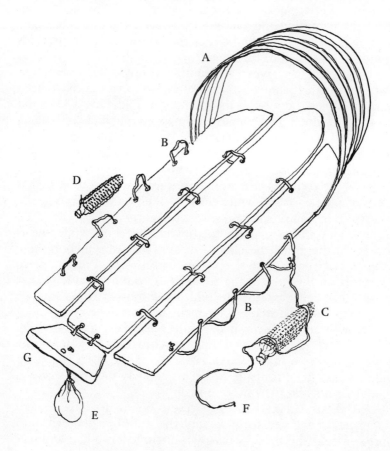

3. LAGUNA PUEBLO Cradle Board

changed. It's a bottle-fed community now, although there is beginning to be a revival of interest in the cradle board and breast-feeding among our younger people.

VICTOR SARRACINO: There is an interesting comparison that can be drawn between the cradle board and the crib and playpen used by the white man. My mother was comparing them one day in terms of discipline. I became quite interested. She said, "Well, we begin by tying you up when you are a child. We feel that discipline begins here. In other words, we need to control your body, not only discipline your mind. This has a significant effect. You're tied up with all these beautiful things, you're not free to move about, therefore you lie peaceful and still. If we left you in these open cribs, you'd begin to kick and feel free. You'd begin to want to move about on your own, and when this happened, we'd have no control over you any more. Even if we said 'no' or 'don't,' you'd follow your own wishes. Somebody might come along and shake that rattle and you'd get all excited and hop about, whereas on a cradle board that rattle would simply put you to sleep, or it would wake you up." So the Indians feel the cradle board is good not only for posture, but also for discipline and control.

In later years, even when I went into the Service or out into society, I remembered all these things. Although I didn't know about the discipline of being in the Service, it helped me along.

ALLEN QUETONE: At our Denver conference, we discussed the net result of the type of Indian training that makes for a more disciplined and less openly competitive child. You have the non-Indian child playing in his crib or playpen, while the Indian child is bound to his cradle. So what do you get when both are in the first grade? You have a quiet and unaggressive Indian, and I think just the opposite non-Indian child. Some may say this is the reason certain Indians do not learn as fast as their non-Indian peers, and why we have such a high dropout rate. I suspect that it is more that our discipline is not geared to what the school system demands.

There is, however, an apparent paradox in the ideal rearing of an Indian child. In terms of present mores and standards, the Indian is taught conflicting values. On the one hand, he is

28

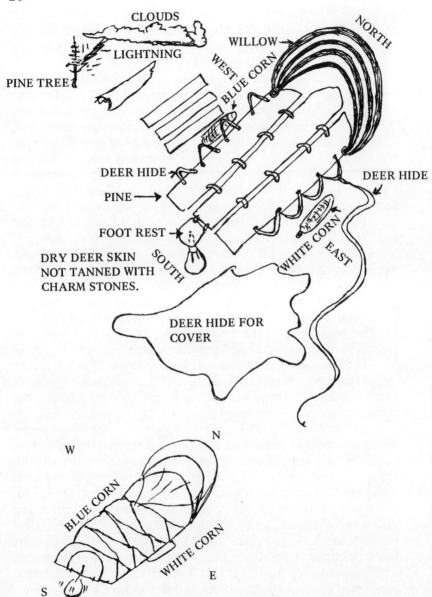

4. Pictorial story of LAGUNA PUEBLO Cradle Board
   as drawn by Victor Sarracino

taught to be self-disciplined; on the other hand, he is taught to be brave, aggressive, and to fight for the things he holds dear.

SYLVESTER MOREY: I don't think there is a paradox here. Quiet, self-disciplined Indians, like yourself, who have learned to use bravery to fight their way through life by means of inner self-control don't drop out of school or society. I would say that the likely dropout is the young Indian who didn't get the traditional training you men are talking about. The young Indian who is cut off from his heritage is the one who can't cope with the situation.

JOHN GARDNER: The importance that all of you place on obedience and control surely isn't for the purpose of making Indians hang onto their mother's apron strings, and of making them dependent and unfree. You are brought up to follow an ideal, and discipline and obedience are part of that ideal and a means of achieving it. Strength and courage appear to be among the qualities the Indian most admires in a man. To achieve both you must be capable of mastering yourself; you must also be willing to submit to and obey what is higher and greater than you are, whether it is your parent when you are a child, or the dictates of your conscience when you are a man.

Let's suppose you are a man. Let's suppose you encounter danger and pain, but that you deal with it in a manly way. What enables you to do this; what are you held by? You are held by your faithfulness to the ideal, by your sense of what a real man ought to do. This ideal has binding power over you. A white child, on the other hand, who has been free to kick and cry as a baby will kick and cry more readily than you when he is confronted by danger and pain as a man. He may not think this is a very ideal way to act, but he is unable to control himself. To begin with, he is not as thoroughly trained in discipline and obedience as you are. Moreover, the ideal toward which the white child should grow has become dim and confused in recent years, and in many instances it has been given up altogether. The ideal has lost its strength and therefore has no power over him. Aren't these some of the crucial differences between us?

4

THE POWER
OF THE WORD

HENRY OLD COYOTE: From the moment a child begins
to speak, he is taught to respect the word; he is taught how to
use the word and how not to use it. The word is all-powerful,
because it can build a man up, but it can also tear him down.
That's how powerful it is. So a child is taught to use words
tenderly and never against anyone; a child is told never to take
anyone's name or reputation in vain.

Every Indian tribe like the Arapahos, the Pueblos, the
Navajos and our friends the Mohawks up New York way, has a
story or legend of creation. The Crow story of creation goes
something like this: The most important element for the Indian
is 'ir; it is inside of us and it surrounds us. In the beginning, the
Supreme Being, or First Person as he is called among my people,
took a piece of earth and formed it into the image of man. He
breathed into this image and brought it to life, and the air that
He breathed into man is the same air that is with us today. The
power of the air is this: it is emptied into the human body, and
it comes out in words and songs that other people can
understand. The First Person breathed into man and man
breathed out the word.

The older people usually tell us, "If you have ways that are
not honorable, such as stretching the truth and spreading
untruths about other people or yourself, there will be times

when people will see you coming and will say, 'Here comes that man! Get the children and women out of the way, because he's going to say something that will be unpleasant to hear!' Then again, you may have emotions that you can't control; you may go to visit somebody and allow your emotions to get the best of you. If you use harsh words, you bring a bad feeling to that home. That person may have been happy when you arrived, but by using words that are unpleasant to hear you spoil his happiness. So if you go into another person's home, try to control your emotions; try to use nice words, so that you don't mar that person's day."

JOHN GARDNER: Nowadays it is often difficult for white parents to know how to talk to their children. They tend either to talk baby talk, to talk down to them, or they draw them into the type of conversations children shouldn't be in on, and then try to explain and reason with them in a very adult manner. How do the Indians speak to their children?

VICTOR SARRACINO: The Pueblos have three stages of language: one for children up to approximately age 9, one for subteens and teenage children, and one for adults. Let me draw a diagram to illustrate what I mean. You have two boys and a girl. If they are all related, the girl will say to this boy who is her brother, "That is my brother," and the second boy will say the same thing in English, "That is my brother." In our language, a girl in the youngest age group will say, "Aw-wa," meaning, "That is my brother." And the second boy in the same age group will say, "Domo." It means the same thing, "That is my brother," but one belongs to the female language and the other to the male language. As they grow a little older, say in their subteens, the boy will address his brother with the word, "Dumo," again meaning, "That is my brother," and the girl will say, "Awwa." When they are adults, the woman will say, "Scha Wa" and the man will say, "Schmo." In the English language it means, "That is my brother" in each case, but the Pueblos have a variety of ways of expressing the same thing. They have a male and a female language, and they have three stages of these two languages, which correspond to the different age groups.

A funny thing happened. There was a priest at Laguna who

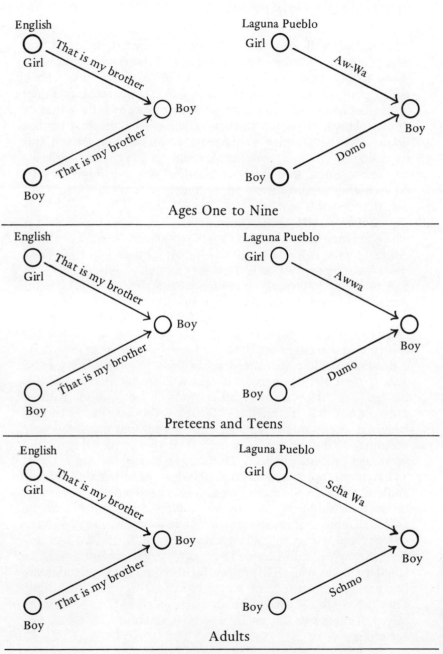

Ages One to Nine

Preteens and Teens

Adults

Three Stages of Language

learned our language from a lady, so that he was speaking the way a woman does. It sounded pretty funny. It also sounds strange if an adult is talking to a child in the adult's language — it just doesn't sound right for the reason that young kids talk the 'kid's' language. I've heard some of the very young who live with their grandparents speak the adult language, and this, too, is quite amusing. And recently there were two cases where a young child was in with the adults during one of our family discussions, and people were really surprised at the way that child spoke the adult language.

HENRY OLD COYOTE: I can appreciate what Vic is saying because of a man I know whom you would consider a man's man. He was in the Second World War; his boat was torpedoed and he spent about 18 hours at sea before he was rescued. He was a man's man because he saw action. He had left the reservation when he was young and went about his business in various parts of the country, then he came back and got married within the tribe. But he had to learn the language as well as the dialect all over again. What he picked up was from his wife, so his expressions are those of a woman. Although he was considered a man's man, he sounds feminine when he speaks. To give you an example, the sound of disbelief that a woman uses is "heeee-hee hee," whereas the man says, "hey hey" in disbelief. "Ugh," the old Hollywood expression that the Indian is supposed to use, is a kind of nonsense. So I can appreciate what Vic is saying, because I've experienced it myself.

The Crow Indians do not have a child's *versus* an adult's language as such. In other words, there are no differences in grammatical structure or basic vocabulary. Nonetheless, we do use language to maintain the distinction between adult and child and also to make the child aware of his or her progress toward maturity. In direct address, for example, the child is called by a word that means, "Dear little boy," or "Dear little girl," progressing to "Dear young man" or "Dear young Lady" at the appropriate age. The progress of a boy or girl from childhood to adulthood is similarly conveyed through the content of what is said. The Crow child is reminded of his or her maturation and corresponding responsibility by phrases

such as "Since you are old now. . . " Also, boys are shaped
toward physical endurance and fortitude by being told, "You're
a man. Act as one."

In my own case, until I had reached puberty, my
grandfather made me feel my age before he addressed me. Then
after puberty, I was a man. That's when he opened the lines of
communication. He told me why people do certain things, and
he told me what to look for and expect in life. You might call it
man-to-man talk and he made certain that I remembered what
he said. He made me feel that I was a man and I was very proud
that he no longer addressed me as a child but considered me as
his equal when he talked to me. My grandfather was considered
a leader of men. By his talking to me as an equal I didn't feel
that I was being over-rated or anything: he was talking to me
from his true feelings, and this had a profound effect on me. I
later discovered that when I talked frankly with my nephew, I
was using the same system.

JOHN GARDNER: It is so difficult to translate from one
culture into another. You speak about the fact that at a certain
moment in your life, your grandfather stopped addressing you
as a child and started talking to you as a man, explaining things
to you and telling you what the reasons for things were. If you
were to translate this without caution from your culture into
our culture, you would not come out with the right answer,
because you also said that he spoke from the heart – and I
imagine that he spoke briefly and pungently and with some
kind of vivid picture. But primarily he spoke in a heartfelt
manner, whereas nowadays we tend to speak with much
reasoning and many words and to convey the kind of
information you might get out of a book. What we express
doesn't especially come from the heart; it comes from the head.
And the more you explain that way, the more of a burden it is
to the child. You're not really strengthening him. To say that
you speak as an adult and give explanations and reasons means
two different things in our two cultures. In one case, it makes a
real man out of you and gives you power; in the other case, it
takes away your power to a large extent.

HENRY OLD COYOTE: What you say is true. I
mentioned earlier that we believe language has a certain power.

By addressing a child as a man when he is ready for it, you help him to become a man. The same is true of names; names carry a certain power. My wife's dad, for example, used to call his children 'Grandpa' and 'Grandma.' By doing that he was making a wish that they would become accustomed to that word and would live to be a grandpa and a grandma.

As a child goes along, maybe he is sickly. Some people will be invited in, and it's up to them to change his name. By changing his name, they hope to change his luck for the better. If a child is healthy, he may keep his name for a long time; but if he starts having bad luck or something, they may decide to change it — not the name he uses to register in at school, but his Indian name.

If a boy goes along and, with the help of his parents or some uncle, does something that is really outstanding, he deserves to inherit the name of someone such as a granduncle. So they give him that new name. I never realized why they did that until I was given the name of a granduncle some time ago. I was given this name when I went into the Service. The reason it was given to me is that this granduncle was the only one known to defend his brother. It is our custom for our brothers to fend for themselves, whereas the respect we have for our sisters extends to our brothers-in-law. We'd go to our brother-in-law's aid much quicker than to our own brother's. But my granduncle decided to defend his brother when he was in trouble in battle. Now, when my own brother enlisted and went into the Service, I enlisted with him. So I was showing the same colors as that man I hadn't seen. I'd only heard about him, but I inherited his name.

It was up to me to find out about that man, my great-uncle, to find out what kind of personality and principles he had. I discovered that he was a kind man, that he was kind to his people and willing to help and share with them in any way. He was also a brave man and showed good judgment. These are the principles he had, and I try to live by them. I try to control my emotions and try to be careful about how I use my words. I don't want to offend anyone; at the same time, I won't back down from danger. So you can see that inheriting names is one of the controls we have and also one of the aids.

The custom of giving someone the name of a man in our tribal history who had admirable traits — traits of strong character that are ideal — tends to change the character of the person who receives that name. Such a character change took place in my clan brother, Andrew Bird in Ground, when he came back from the Second World War. He had proved himself in battle during the Battle of the Bulge and was decorated for valor, so when he came back his clan uncles got together and decided that he deserved a name that would be fitting for his deeds. He was a clan nephew of Chief Plenty Coups, and so they took the name of Plenty Coups and passed it on to him.

Plenty Coups was a good man. Back in 1921 they brought him to Washington, D.C. along with other chiefs from various tribes for the dedication of the Tomb of the Unknown Soldier. The chiefs themselves selected Plenty Coups to represent the Indian nations, so he was given the title of Chief of all Chiefs. He had the honor of putting his war bonnet and coup stick on the coffin of the Unknown Soldier and because of this, a Presidential Proclamation came out that the war bonnet was part of the uniform of the American Indian and needn't be shed in the passing of the Colors or the playing of the National Anthem.

Now Andrew Bird in Ground was a rascal and had rough ways. He was just about as rough as I was, maybe rougher; but from the time he inherited that name, he changed his ways. It was up to him to live by the principles of the old Chief Plenty Coups and he controlled himself. He was very quiet. He even abstained from alcoholic beverages, because you never know what you might do when you're under the influence of alcohol; you're not in your best judgment. So he had good advice, and now the people respect him.

Later on during the conflict in Vietnam, my nephew, my brother's boy, was over there and was decorated for valor. When he came back, Andrew, who is this boy's clan uncle, decided to pass his name on to him. When Andrew first received the name, he did some checking on the background of the Chief and found out that the name Plenty Coups had never been in jail. It was up to him to teach my nephew about Chief Plenty Coups and to alert him to the fact that that name had never been in jail. Whatever he did, he was told to keep that name out of jail!

If we do something as we grow up that warrants a change in name, those people that we respect, the clan uncles, take us out and announce that they are going to change our name and that we are to be known by a new name from that day on. Well, I was on the rough side just like Andrew — not slightly on the rough side but very much so. I enjoyed facing danger as something that challenged my bravery; I didn't want to let other people know I had any fear at all. But after I had inherited the new name I mentioned earlier, and started checking up on my great granduncle who had held it before me, I found out that he was one of the signers of the Treaty of 1851. He must have been a good man to sign a treaty on behalf of his people. And, like I said, I found out that he had a strong character and never backed down from danger but at the same time he was a kind person and considerate. He had a kind word for everyone, especially for children, and most of the children that he came into contact with had a lot of respect for him.

And so I try to live by these principles, even with women. If you are a man, you should never lay a hand on a woman or do her bodily harm; your body is so much stronger than hers. And if you feel like taking something out on a person because of anger, you should channel your energy to something more useful. My grandfather on my mother's side told me that when your blood boils and you start getting mad about something, all you need is a little patience and a little self-control. If you breathe deeply four times, you will soon forget what you were cranky about. So I try to do this. Even though I might disagree with my wife, I'd never strike her. Because if I wanted to strike something, I'd rather get satisfaction from striking something hard. Then again, my wife might turn the tables on me. . . .

As I was growing up, I remembered certain elders for their good traits. And today I still remember something good about the different people I knew. I may also remember certain things that are unfortunate about a person, but I try not to think about these. I think about the good in a person, because that's the way people look at me and I try not to disappoint them.

The giving of the second name usually takes place at adolescence when a boy becomes a man, just as the childhood name is given shortly after birth. When I was born I was given a name — come to think of it, I should sue the City of Billings for stealing my Indian name, "Big Sky." After I grew up a little bit, something like a bringing out party was held and I was given my second name. This was when I entered manhood. Now, if a young man does something outstanding and has shown that he could be a future leader or future defender of his people, he is brought out for recognition and the clan decides to change his second name to something new. Later on, he may go out and distinguish himself by giving away something of value or doing something good in the eyes of the people, so they rename him again. Still later, someone may decide that he deserves a new name, and as he continues to do good deeds, the people may continue to change his name.

An Indian is always known by his most recent name; in some cases, however, the immediate family may choose to make an exception and continue to call him by his first given name. I'm Henry Old Coyote to white people, but to my own people I am known as the "One Who Was Wounded in the Draw." When you inherit a name, you still can keep the name you had unless someone asks for it and gives you a gift in exchange. You can give your name away, in other words, if you inherit a new one. I'm on my seventh name now.

ALLEN QUETONE: When somebody was given a name, my people had a ceremony, and a man made an announcement to the camp that henceforth this person was to be called so and so. Like Henry said, these names are honorable because of the men who held them before; they're not given out helter-skelter. If a man possesses qualities that were close to an honorable man in the past, then he earns that man's name. Not long ago I went to some naming ceremonies, and they still go through the traditional ritual: the announcement of this person's new name and of the fact that people may always depend on him for this or that. If anybody from the tribe ever calls on him for some particular help, that man has an obligation to help in order to live up to his name. It's a great honor to be given such a name.

My great-grandfather had four wives, and as a result we have four family lines that all have a right to his name. But nobody has it yet; nobody has made a move. There has to be some kind of agreement by all the family groups as to who is going to get it. If it's handled properly, the name should go to the family that has the boy or man who comes closest to what our great-grandfather was.

VICTOR SARRACINO: In raising a child, we feel that language is of prime importance in getting the child to establish a behavior pattern. After marriage, and even before marriage, young women are taught to sing many lullabies and songs so that they will use these songs after the child is born. My people claim that this is one of the ways women start to develop a child's mind — the child's mind is formed through hearing the words of its language.

HENRY OLD COYOTE: Speaking of lullabies, we Indians have lullabies about animals and how they have a tenderness toward their offspring. These lullabies have been passed on from generation to generation, and are still being sung today. There is one about a mother horse singing to her colt — she describes the little colt when he is trotting, how his mane is shaking and how he has to be careful about what his tail touches. He's got long hairs and is not the prettiest thing, but still he's the loved one. Another is about a sow bear singing to her cub — the baby bear's got small eyes and keeps running under the bank. We sing about the little buck deer the first time he has horns — he's going to shed his horns but the mother tells him they'll grow back. "Don't worry," she says, "You're a lively one, you're a frisky one; your antlers will grow back."

Some of these lullabies also give a. clue to where we come from, where we've been. We sing about Chief Mountain. This lullaby describes the area below Chief Mountain; there are pine trees there, and in that patch of timber are some cattails where the enemy was at one time. We sing about the Canadian River. The Crow Indians call it the Arrowhead River. That's where the ravens come, just to the south of that river, which gives us the clue that the Crows were down that way. So when the child hears these lullabies and stories, he is made aware. When they sing about the Arrowhead River, the child begins to wonder, and as he grows up, he tries to find out where the river is. At least, that's the way I was. The first trip I took down to Oklahoma, the Arrowhead River was the first thing I looked for and wanted to see.

The principal thing children are taught by hearing these lullabies is respect. They are taught to respect certain things in life and certain people. By giving respect, they hope to gain self-respect and through self-respect, they gain the respect of others. Self-respect is one of the qualities my people stress and try to nurture, and one of the controls an Indian has as he grows up. Once you lose your self-respect, you just go down.

ERNEST BENEDICT: Among my people, not only lullabies but stories play a very important role in instructing children. Fall and winter are storytelling time, the time of legends. During the summer, I guess, children are expected to be much too busy and active for stories, and anyway, by the time it gets dark, it's bedtime.

The real old legends that still survive almost always have a moral. Many of them are about various birds and animals and are meant to teach children about virtues and faults. The story of how the robin got his red breast, for example, really tells you how to take care of birds and animals, and how you should try to treat them almost as people, as guests. It's actually an Iroquois story, and I think it's even been written in books.

Then there's the story of the rabbit who wanted to show off. He was showing how fast and how long he could run. He ran so long that eventually it began snowing and the snow got packed underneath him and lifted him way up. It snowed and snowed and soon he found himself up in the branches of the trees. So he jumped into a tree and fell asleep. While he was sleeping, the snow melted and there he was still up in that tree. Since he had no claws with which to climb down, he eventually had to jump out of the tree. His tail and ears got caught in a branch so that his ears stretched way out and his tail got permanently stuck up there. Then he fell and hit his nose against a sharp object and split his face. That explains his split nose and his stretched-out ears and why his tail comes out every spring in the pussy willows. And so a lesson is learned about showoffs and smart alecks.

Some of these stories are purely for entertainment. Then, of course, there are the tall stories, some of which have been modernized. For instance, a man was telling about how well he tended his garden. He got a potato out of it that was big enough to fill a wheelbarrow. So another man says, "I got one so big that when I dug it up out of the garden, I hit it with a shovel and it sounded hollow. So I cut a hole and got down inside of it and found another garden in it with a potato field!"

These are some of the stories that are told during the winter. Children are usually encouraged to stay up. The evenings start early and are long, and so the children can stay up and listen to them. Now that I look back on it, the grownups would rather have been doing something else, but they told stories for the benefit and entertainment of the kids, and it was through these stories that we learned many things. Even the tall tales contained a lesson. Youngsters were shown that a lie is so ridiculous that you shouldn't give it any belief at all, that it isn't worthy of serious thought. So we received a kind of moral teaching through our legends and tales.

5
FOUNDATION
OF THE EARLY YEARS

HENRY OLD COYOTE: If we follow the child to the next stage of his growth, we come to the time when he is teething. Nowadays you have plastic and celluloid teething rings, but back in the old days the Indians used gristle or the udder of Buffalo. The Indians, you might say, invented pacifiers before the white man even thought of them. In the old days, when the mother was busy putting up the tipi and taking care of it, she used to take the udder of a buffalo cow, pierce it with a stick, and give it to the child to suck on. Or she gave him a piece of gristle which is rich in fat and helped the child put on weight and keep healthy.

One of the high points of the child's early years is when he takes his first step. The grandmother makes Indian pudding and feeds the parents and other relatives who happen to be there at that moment. As they partake of the pudding, they make wishes for the child to take many more steps. You might call it prayers to the unknown that the child will take many more steps in the future.

As far as childhood diseases are concerned, if there happens to be an epidemic, the Indian will go to a fire, take dried grass and put it in a circle; he will let the child stand in the center and then he will burn that grass. The circle of fire is supposed to prevent the disease from infecting the child. There are many cases where this has worked, even today. My wife's sister is one of those who has the ability to perform this service and she has cured a number of illnesses this way.

Quite often our Indian remedies are more effective than the white man's. I remember one instance when a white doctor gave up on a child. He had diagnosed the illness as spinal meningitis, but as it turned out, it was nothing but common colic and this child had a sore spine. My wife's sister is one of those people who has the right to massage a person to help overcome that soreness in the neck and cure the colic. There is a certain way to massage so that the soreness goes away and the person gets well.

So I have seen several occasions where a white doctor would give up on a child and an Indian woman would take this child home and care for him and cure him. My sister-in-law is younger than my wife but she has that right. My wife has different capacities. She's in the process of inheriting a remedy for sore mouth and sore throats, but first she has to prove herself. Since she is the eldest child, she's entitled to inherit this from her uncle. If she had an older brother, he would be entitled to it, but as the eldest, she's in line for it and she's being checked out now. There are certain things she has to do and certain things she has to look for. If she gets blessings from that Super Power and is receptive, she may become one of those people who can cure this particular ailment. She'll be fasting come the second of July.

MAX HANLEY: To follow along with the child, after the baby is three or four months old, there will be the first laugh. I don't know how the baby makes the first laugh. Maybe someone tickles her, or maybe children are playing, or a little kitten. Anyway, something makes the baby laugh the first laugh; it's an important occasion and calls for a celebration. Maybe the people kill a sheep, cut it up and make a little sauce to go with it; then they build a big fire and start to roast this meat. Sometimes they sing songs for the baby, because they wish to teach the child, this boy or girl, not to be selfish, not to be stingy with anything.

When the child is about four or five years old, he's got to be taught, he's got to begin to learn about things. I remember three things when I was four years old, and when I was five, my mother says, "Son, you are five years old now. You must count each year as the years go by." So I started counting from the time I was five years old, and I'm still counting — I never forget. This coming September 25, I'll count to 74, and I started at five.

As the youngster grows up, the boy or girl starts herding sheep or learning how to approach a horse or donkey. Sometimes the horse kicks, or the donkey is hard to approach, so they learn how you touch the nose a little bit, then put the rope around the neck. They learn how you kind of go easy when you ride. This is horsemanship. When you put the saddle on the horse's back in the morning, you don't ride right off; you have to go easy and trot about half a mile at first, then you can go off at a gallop. That's the way these youngsters are trained.

VICTOR SARRACINO: Children at the age of four and thereafter become great actors. The old folks claim that this is the time to establish a good foundation, because from the fourth year on, kids begin to learn many things that will stay in their memories for many years to come. As we always say, everything begins at four — it's a kind of magical number, so at age four we feel it's highly important to teach the child as many things as we can, as many of the old Indian ways. I don't know how old I was, but I remember being told a great deal that I still cherish and to this day pass on to my own children.

Most of our children, even today, are initiated when they are four into the Indian way of life. They are taught their traditions. When the youngster is first initiated, he is given a bath in rain water. At this time, a circle of hair is cut from the center of the child's head, just like your monks. It's cut close; right now it's done with scissors but it used to be done with a knife. We feel that this is where the rain gods will take hold of the child and give him wisdom and all those things we pray about. This hair is taken up into a mountain and buried. Thereafter, any hair that is cut is burned. The first haircut has a religious purpose, but every time we cut hair thereafter, we ask the Supreme God for forgiveness, because we are destroying something that grows from nature. That's why we burn it — so that it will turn back into ashes and go back into the earth.

After the first hair is cut, we attach the fluffy kind of eagle feather to the child's head. At the end of the fourth day, we remove the feather and take it to a hilltop and place it at the very tip of an evergreen tree. It has to be a perfect tree, with no broken branches or anything. After we clean around the trunk, we place the feather on the highest point of the tree, because we believe that this feather serves as a messenger to the Supreme Being and carries the message of all the prayers for the child that have been said, prayers that he may have a fruitful and long life like the trees of the forest, and the kind of farsightedness you have from the vantage of that treetop. At this moment, the youngster makes a pledge to forever protect all things of nature: the animals, the plants, the air, and all that the individual may come into contact with that is of nature. From this time on, the child is allowed to participate in all social and ceremonial dances.

Soon afterwards the child is permitted to enter the kiva* for the first time. On this occasion, a second set of parents is established, and it is they who sponsor the child and are responsible for giving him guidance in ceremonies and any religious activities. The child is then given a second name that blends in with the clan of his sponsors. As a result, the youngster is accepted into the sponsor's family and is treated just like one of its members, like a brother or sister. Then the name is sanctioned in a ceremony where an ear of white corn and an ear of blue corn are offered and the ceremony is repeated four times; in other words, the child accepts the name four times, and so do the others. Along with the two ears of corn, the youngster is presented with gifts like mocassins and other things he might need as he participates in the old traditional dances and festivities. Then many other things are given by relatives of the sponsoring parents. They all line up with gifts, and it gives you a wonderful feeling as it takes place.

Kids have a lot of imagination; anything you tell them seems to materialize in their minds. I remember that they used to take us down to the creek to learn how to swim, and I guess I

---

*In the Pueblo culture, a room devoted to secret religious ceremonies, tribal councils, etc.. The room is entered by an opening in the roof. *Ed.*

Boys jumping over bushes

overdid it, because if they wanted me, that's where they found me — down at the creek. My mother was telling me that one day when I was little, I came home and wanted to eat dinner. I was rushing her and she asked me why I was in such a hurry to get back. I'd seen these pictures of mermaids and so I guess I told her, "Well, there's a mermaid waiting for me down at the creek!" They always tease me about this, particularly since I'm a member of the Water Clan.

As kids we never knew when the ceremonial or religious dances were coming, but we often used to go outside and lay some dirt on the ground and wet it down. Then we'd put our feet on it, hoping that the dances would bring us a pair of shoes if we'd been good, and that our footprints would show exactly what size we wore. Or we would make something out of clay like a horse and take it to a place of shrine, and pray that we would receive a real horse in later years.

During my childhood we did a lot of foot-racing and climbing. And like anybody else, we chased butterflies. In those days our parents made baskets. They would tell us to go out and chase a butterfly, catch it, and bring it back so that they could copy the design on its wings and weave the pattern into the basket. So that's what we did — we chased butterflies and we chased grasshoppers. For good health they used to tell us, "After you get through hoeing the fields and cutting the weeds, try to see if you can run along the irrigation ditch as you come home. If you want to take a short cut, jump over the bushes, don't go around them. See if you can jump the bushes as you come home!" So chasing butterflies and jumping ditches was not only for fun, but for physical fitness as well.

In my day we used to make a lot of arrows and did a lot of hunting down at the creek, shooting at fish and all that. But we were always told never to kill a water snake or even a frog. In fact, this is what some of the old folks used to tell us: "Be careful about messing around with water snakes. If you want to find out what we mean, get down to the creek and grab as many fish as you can from under the rocks and put them in sacks; grab three or four water snakes and put them in the sacks, too, then dump them back in the pond and jump in." I don't know whether they were daring us or what, but we used to do that.

All summer long we'd be grabbing these water snakes and fish;
then we'd throw them back into the water and dive in with
them. It gives you a funny feeling when the snakes start chasing
you. You're just being playful with them and there's not much
harm, but it scares you all the same.

Rather than always running to the store, we made our own
toys as kids. We made whistles, we made little darts, we made
arrows that we thought we'd never see again when they went up
in the air. We'd take a corncob and put a nail at one end and
bird feathers at the other end and then we'd throw the cob
around. It was lots of fun to see who could throw it furthest.
Then we'd cut strips from cornstalks and make little birds out
of the cobs with cornstalk wings and we'd see who could make
the prettiest one. We also used to see who could make the best
horses out of clay and the best pottery.

We were taught many things. To give you an example, we
were told that when we heard that first thunder in spring, we
should start stretching out, and start looking forward to a great
year. But we were also taught that we should never stretch
while eating, because if we did, the wind would get the
nourishment that was intended for us. This was probably to
make us better behaved at meals, but there could be many
interpretations for what we were told.

Even at an early age they would take us out into the corn
fields and into the wide open range and tell us which plants to
use at different times and different seasons. I got a chance to
learn about many plants, and though I couldn't tell you what
their proper names are — because to this day I've never looked
into a book to see what they are called scientifically — I know
that I could go out there and point them out to you and tell
you what they can be used for. Now I take my own kids out
and teach them what I learned, and they really enjoy it.

In times past, there was never any smoking or any drinking
of alcoholic beverages. In fact, the only people who used to
smoke were the leaders of various societies, and only at the time
of religious ceremonies. Smoking really had a special time and
place, and if you did not belong to any of the societies, you
were not supposed to smoke at all. My grandfather belonged to
one of those societies whose job it was to go out during the year

and cut wheat and gather in corn. The family volunteered to go along and help, but before we began, each of us had to take a puff of a cigarette to consecrate our work. I was a small kid and it was the only time I ever smoked. It allowed me to join in the group and do what they were doing, in other words, working with their hands and pulling off the corn. It was a great privilege, because we were taught at an early age that everything is sacred and anything that grows from the ground is a nourishment which goes into the human being from the body of mother earth. Anyway, they used to tell us youngsters that smoking was not good for our lungs or for our body, and that we shouldn't smoke until we could run down a coyote and grab it by the tail. Now, everyone knows that it's next to impossible to catch a coyote by running!

So we didn't have too much idle time as kids, and it seems to me that I was young for a long time. I thought I would never grow up, and people still tell me that I look pretty young. I feel young and I appreciate it. I was telling my wife the other day that it seems as if I was a kid for a long time; it seems there was no end to my childhood. And I have to say that I've certainly enjoyed life so far!

HENRY OLD COYOTE: Among the Crow Indians, children are encouraged to play games and enjoy life, and many of these games prepare them for later responsibilities. Little boys, for example, are given a rope or something that resembles a weapon; they are also encouraged to begin learning about certain animals and birds. The girls will probably play house, and this is where their instruction comes in. They do a little sewing, and they learn how to make dolls and how to prepare food. In other words, they are being prepared for later life, but in a manner that is natural and fun.

As they get a little older, boys are trained for fitness and survival. They do a lot of running and start by chasing butterflies. The older people tell them that if they catch a butterfly and rub it on their chest, they are going to be good runners. I never realized what I was doing until I grew older, and then I saw how much running I was getting in and how much strength I had built up!

Back in the old days before my time, my people would kill

"There's a man in that hole"

a buffalo bull, take a piece of its heart and give it to the boy to eat. By eating that heart, the boy was supposed to develop courage and a strong heart, because a buffalo bull goes forward all the time — it never backs down. Even in death, it falls forward; the same is true of a bear. So when a boy gets hurt, he doesn't cry. Instead, he makes a whiffing sound in imitation of that buffalo or bear — 'Shuh!' He feels the pain but he doesn't cry, he doesn't carry on. He remembers that he has a piece of that heart in him and he wouldn't cry if it killed him — it's only little girls that cry.

Another practice that toughens young boys is taking a cold dip in a river or creek as soon as they get up in the morning. In the winter my people used to cut a hole in the ice and tell the youngsters, "There's a man in that hole who has a bow and arrow and he's waiting for you. If you don't give him a chance to shoot that arrow, you'll be all right." By taking cold dips in the fall and all through the winter they became acclimatized to it and never caught cold. But if they hesitated, and that man shot the arrow, they got pneumonia. Nowadays young people don't do it any more. There's a loss of parental control, and we're also learning the white man's way and making it too convenient — we all have bathrooms and running water.

MAX HANLEY: What you've just described reminds me of why the Navajos live to be between 80 and 90. When we were little, we had to roll in the snow at the first snow in the fall, and then go back home where there was a big fire to warm up. We had to do this four separate times. Or we had to stand under a tree that was full of snow and shake it on ourselves. This was the worst, and if you didn't do it right away, your grandfather would grab you, pull you under that tree, and shake it hard. Boy, every time I went under there, I cried. But that's the way they made us tough, and it helped us to live until a good old age. We also had to run three or four miles to the east and back, early every morning. We had to get up and run, run, run here and there, and in the process we looked for berries way out in the woods and along the creek. We also chased deer and other wild animals. The old traditional people used to tell us: "One of these days the enemy may try to attack you. Now, if you are one of those who sleeps late, after the sun comes up, and you

try to run, the enemy will be able to shoot you with a single
arrow; you'll be lying down with just one feathered arrow
sticking out of your *back*. On the other hand, if you are one of
those who runs early in the morning, rolls in the snow and
shakes snow on yourself, you will be really tough. If the enemy
overcomes you, people will find you with half a dozen good
arrows in your *chest*. Warriors will inspect the number of good
arrows in your chest, because that's the way they used to judge
a man's toughness and strength, and they'll say, 'Ah, this
person must have been a really tough guy. He must have been
running here and there early in the morning. That's the kind of
person we like to see.' " That's what I was told. You see, it took
quite a few arrows to bring that strong man down; and he
wasn't running away, he was running to meet the enemy's
challenge.

ARTHUR SUTTON: Now, I'm going to tell you this one
thing that I was taught. You had to get up early in the morning
in the winter time, go down to the creek, cut a hole in the ice
and let your grandfather throw you in. That's one of the ways
you got trained for survival. Another thing: in the cold
morning, Grandfather calls my name and says, "Get up and
come eat breakfast!" I knew good and well that he didn't have a
fire started, so I didn't pay any attention. So he comes to the
place where I was sleeping, gets me up and walks me outside.
There's a big old snowdrift there, so he just throws me in.
"That's where you belong. You sleep too late. Now get up, go
out there and tend to the horses." So I got my clothes on and
went out. That's how I began to learn how to ride horses and
take care of them. I rode riding horses and I rode broncs. I
didn't care how many times they threw me off, I got back on.
Now, how many among the younger element can take care of
horses today, or for that matter, take care of anything?
Nowadays Indian kids no longer go through this kind of early
training.

6
SLEEPING
AND WAKING

ALLEN QUETONE: I think it's a universal trait among children that they want to stay up, and it's a parental or grandparental chore to get them to bed. We had a set routine at bedtime and there were reasons behind it. I can remember that my grandfather used to tell me legends at night and he always wanted me to say, 'Hah!' This is a sign that you're listening while storytelling is going on. He told me to keep saying 'Hah' while he was telling me these tales, the idea being that whenever he stopped hearing me say it, I was asleep.

But I think this moment, this very short moment before falling asleep is the most likely period for learning. This is when they tell you stories to build character, to build morality, because all these legends and tales have little things, little morals tied up in them. And I guess they tell them at the right moment, because they stay in your mind at that time and sink in when you go to sleep.

Something that ties in with the period prior to sleep is the effort to create in the child an awareness of the spirit in the old Indian way. They used to tell us stories that scared the daylights out of us, and I often wondered why. I used to think it was simply to scare kids — that, at least, is what they accomplished — but as I get older I think it was principally to make children aware that there are spirits or powers out there. The stories they told were related to ghosts, to power, to fear. One of my most vivid memories was the stories about the owl, because the owl is the one bird in our tradition that is a bad omen, and hearing about him used to have a frightening effect. These stories and legends instilled an awareness in us that there is something bigger than yourself. It was a kind of childlike awareness, because at that time all I knew was that I was just plain scared; but it marked the first stage of my belief in a higher power.

HENRY OLD COYOTE: Before the youngster goes to sleep, the grandparents will sing some songs and explain their meaning and significance; they'll also tell legends that are meant to help build character, or tell a story where somebody pulled a blunder. All of these things work on the child when he is asleep. I've been trying to remember some of the bedtime stories I heard as a boy. I try to practice these stories on my wife in order to refresh my memory, but she tells me, "Keep quiet; I want to sleep!"

It's all right for a child to sleep because he needs the rest, but the moment of waking is a significant time. Come the early morning, my grandfather would always tell me, "It's all right to sleep, but now you have had your rest. Sleep is not your ally; sleep is not your friend. Rise up early with the sun and face a new day. If you rise up early enough, you'll be lucky. Face that Old Man!" meaning the sun. "He sees you and he's going to give you something. Face a new day — it's just like being born again!" These are some of the sayings he had. He would tell me, "You can't return to yesterday. You have to keep going forward." That's why we have the tipi facing east and why we turn to the right when we go out, because that's the path we have to take in order to face the sun, the Old Man, who is going round and round.* "When the different birds arise, they are enjoying a new day. Enjoy the new day with these others from the forest. With all the living creatures around, your brothers, face a new day!" This is the way my grandfather would greet me in the morning. He made me realize that by joining in when the birds are rejoicing and singing songs of happiness, I could share in that good feeling and retain it through the day.

JOHN GARDNER: So the rising stories unite you with the

---

*Cf. Chapter 11, P. 118, for a further explanation of this practice.

environment of the new day, whereas the going-to-sleep ones have a more inner character and give you wisdom and a moral teaching.

HENRY OLD COYOTE: Yes, the bedtime stories encourage you to sleep and think about something that will strengthen you. At the same time, we make a wish for the child to have a dream; a good dream, not a bad one. This parallels the expression of the non-Indians to have 'sweet dreams.'

ALLEN QUETONE: I can remember that when my grandfather got up at home early in the morning, he would always say, "Be-hai, be-hai, key-dai-baw-dai." This means, "It's time to get up, it's time to get up. The Old Man is rising!" In other words — get out and greet him! He would say this very enthusiastically and repeat it about two or three times. In camp we have the camp caller who goes around and wakes everybody up and says his ritual prayer, then talks about things in general or tells of coming events. He is like a newspaper, I guess, and he goes around before everybody is awake.

HENRY OLD COYOTE: I will tell you of an experience my brother had when he was a little boy. When he was a year old, he used to take everything off when he was in bed with his grandfather. In the mornings, the old man would get up and build a fire, then grab a blanket and grab my brother. Down to the creek they would go and jump in that hole in the ice. When they came back to the house, there would be icicles in their hair, and he would tell my brother the same thing he had told me, "You're a man. That man with the bow and arrow didn't get us; we're back!"

My grandfather was one of those who had the license or privilege of making the kind of announcements Allen is talking about. Recently, I have been assigned the same thing. In the mornings I am the first one my people hear. I'm up before the sun gets up. I have to make four hollers, which means that I call upon the spirits to come to my aid — the aid of the announcer — so that nothing will mar the proceedings. I tell the people, "It's a good day. It's a good day. The Old Man is coming up. Get up, get up! Drink a lot of water!. Circulate your blood! Face a new day!" These are the expressions I am meant to use. They are not my words or ideas; they are passed on to me and I carry on what the old-timers used to do.

When my grandfather returned from that cold plunge, he would sit back and start singing and no one could sleep then. He would sing scouting songs and victory songs, and lodge songs, and you just couldn't help but listen to them. He made me aware of the songs that deal with the various activities of my people. The same was true of my wife's grandfather. I believe she knows more of those songs than I do, because her grandfather was a great one for singing them. I'm pretty sure she heard them from early morning until breakfast. The only time they would stop was when breakfast was ready.

VICTOR SARRACINO: In our area, we usually sing songs to the youngsters to put them to sleep. Even if the parents have something to do, they will stop everything and lie down with their children and sing to them until they go off to sleep. When I was a kid, my mother and grandparents sang to me until I was in the fifth or sixth grade, and told me about a lot of things that I seem to have remembered and learned. I guess I slept on what I was told.

At night when I have many things to do — and I often have meetings to attend — I still make a point of putting my kids to bed. I lie down with them on each side of me and tell them stories that they really enjoy, and they go off to sleep feeling secure that I've gone to sleep with them. As soon as they are asleep, I sneak out and go about my business; but each day they remember the night before. "Isn't it right, Daddy, that we all went to sleep last night?" they'll say. "Boy, we had a good night's sleep!"

The only significant thing I remember is that we never lie in the same direction as the dead. All the dead lie with their heads facing the rising sun, facing east, and that's the only direction in which we never sleep. We believe that if we do, the dead will sleep with us and that we will therefore be disturbed all night long.

We usually sleep on the ground or floor. I enjoy sleeping on the floor, and I guess I'm one of those individuals who is really used to it, because I've had many falls off a bed. When I went into the Service, I fell out many times, and you know how high those bunks are!

JOHN GARDNER: Certainly the conditions of going to sleep and waking up are very important. I believe the night contains wisdom, and that when we are asleep we are close to wisdom. What value do you place on dreams? Does the Indian believe, as many people do, that when you sleep at night, your spirit leaves your body and that dreams are a remembering of experiences outside your body? You said before that you always want to make certain that the child's spirit comes along when the child travels. Do you believe that the child's spirit also leaves his body at nighttime and lives in a higher, a sacred realm?

HENRY OLD COYOTE: Let's just say that dreams play an important part in a child's development. There are cases where people have dreams and come into contact with a person or object that is not of this world, but they have no proof that they actually left their bodies and made contact with that object or creature or person. We go right back to the Indian belief that there is something out there surrounding you, a force or spirit that can be evil or good. The Crow Indians say that there is a message in everything and that the force we are talking about has a way of communicating with you if you are receptive. Dreams are one of the ways, and this is why we make wishes for a person to have good dreams when he or she goes to sleep.

Sometimes a dream can be a warning. We may have bad dreams about our relatives, so there are certain procedures we go through to pacify that force out there. It's a force we do not understand but we know it exists, like the force of a magnet which you can't see but know is there. There are times when something will occur to you, like an electric shock, and make you more alert. This something may be your subconscious mind, or your guardian angel; but whatever it is, whatever name you have for it, it is there and it tells you certain things both in your waking consciousness and through your dreams. That's why Crow Indians make wishes on their dreams. For example, if you have a vision or dream of grass growing in spring, you make wishes that someone close to you will progress to that time in good health and prosperity. Or you may dream of snow on the ground; all right, you wish that that person will live to see another winter, blessed with an abundance of good things.

7

INSTILLING THE WISH
TO OBEY

JOHN GARDNER: You have presented us with an
interesting paradox. On the one hand, you bring up your
children with rigor so that they are ready to withstand
deprivations and difficulties; on the other hand, you cannot be
too good to them and you load your affections upon them.
How do you reconcile your belief in discipline with your
inclination to be lenient and tender toward your young?

HENRY OLD COYOTE: I have heard the elders say that
you can love your children and grandchildren — they deserve
that love — but you can still be firm with them. The important
thing is to make your kids feel that you care for them and that
you want to give them your attention. In my younger days
when I came home from school or came in from outside, my
grandfather always let me know that he knew I existed. The
minute I stepped inside he would say, "Here comes that man. Is
there any food around here? He may be hungry." He made me
feel I was essential. Or if he had gone out and I happened to be
at home, the first thing he would say when he came in was,
"Where's that man?" On those occasions, he didn't say, 'that
boy,' or use my name; he said 'man,' which made me feel that I
wanted to be a man. I practice the same thing with my niece
and with my little grandchildren. The first thing I say to my
niece when I come home is, "Where's that little woman?

Where's that woman?" At least youngsters get the feeling that we appreciate them and set store by them. At the same time we tell them, "If you do this, you're going to get hurt; if you do that, you're going to feel bad." Today, because we rely on teachers to do this for us, so much of the affection and respect between children and their elders is lost.

ALLEN QUETONE: Since I live very much in the white man's world, I have tried to adapt this practice so that it fits in with the demands of my schedule. When I come home in the evening, I know that my children want to talk to me, and that they each have their own stories to tell. I've got four kids and this runs into a lot of time, especially when you get home late and have to sit through all of it. So instead of taking them one at a time, when I come home I say that I would like to meet with all the little people. This to me is the same Indian way. I am talking to them in a group and I am giving them a chance to talk to me.

HENRY OLD COYOTE: It's surprising what a difference it makes. When I make a point of noticing my niece, she will come up to me and say, "How did everything go today? You and Mama fight? Anyone fight you?" In the process, she will tell me about some problems she didn't have a chance to tell others, so that I'll take care of them. She feels better; she feels a certain amount of security in being noticed.

Some people think they are providing for their children. They provide them with color television, with a record player, and with games of some sort; they get them a Honda. But all of it is done so that the children will stay out of their way. Parents are providing for their children in a selfish manner. But I know, having been a child once, that I liked attention.

One of my nephews was copying the older boys; he had long hair. His brothers wouldn't let him get a haircut because his ears were too big, but his parents finally convinced him that little boys are supposed to look different from little girls and that a lot of people thought he was a girl. So they cut his hair. I had heard that he had had a haircut. He came up to me and wanted to be noticed, but I pretended not to notice him until I looked straight at him. "Hey, who are you? Are you the same one or the other one?" He says, "I was the other one, but I'm

VICTOR SARRACINO and HENRY OLD COYOTE

me now." For that he deserved a dime; I gave him a dime. The next time he was the other one that I knew and said, "I'm me today." So I gave him another dime. I made a little game out of it. I also make a game of noticing my niece. When I come home, I'll say, "Where's Lina? Is she still around or did she go somewhere? Did she go without telling me?" She'll keep quiet. Then she'll hide, and all of a sudden she'll say, "Surprise!" And I'll be surprised, and that's when she tells me her problems. So having been a child myself, I know that I liked to have grownups notice me. I didn't go out of my way and do something to gain attention. They simply made a point of taking notice and this gave me a feeling of security.

The older people tell us, "It doesn't mean much to be deprived of material things because you can always get a replacement, but you can never replace a human life, such as that of a child. So appreciate your young while you have them." By this advice, our elders teach us to appreciate people. One of the ways of showing appreciation is through the attention you give; it is also through listening to the advice of those who love you. My grandfather used to tell me, "In return for the expressions of our love to you, you must show your appreciation in some way. You must obey some instructions, some orders, some commands. If you have no ears for good advice, people won't think much of you. You won't have the respect that other people have. If you have respect, hang on to it." Today that form of instruction is lacking. Kids simply want to be like the others they see. They read about things like demonstrations, which are the 'in' thing and supposedly exciting. They are looking for something to replace what they should have been taught. I believe it's up to the elders to provide that something by teaching them the old ways and by teaching them respect.

VICTOR SARRACINO: One thing I've noticed with kids is that you can never give them enough love. That's what is going to do the trick. My grandparents and parents give all their love to my children and my kids enjoy it and never tire of it. I try to do the same thing, and as a result, my kids and I never tire of each other. Before I figured all of this out, I used to bark at them or even holler at them to correct them, but it never worked. So I had to change my whole system. You shouldn't be mean and you shouldn't be harsh, but you can be firm. In order to discipline a child, you don't have to abuse him. You can deprive him of something he really likes until he promises to abide by what you say.

When we were young, we were taught to have a lot of respect for our elders, especially our grandparents. I didn't realize it until recently, but in order to get us trained, our grandfathers would test us. They would say, "Could you go after that thing and bring it to me?" They were already doing this when we were four, so we grew into it. Even today if they ask me to go after something, I'll go after it. The other day I was telling someone about a boy who never had this upbringing. His father bought a horse that he was going to give him. One day he didn't have time to water it and so he asked the boy, "Son, why don't you water the horse?" That kid answered, "You go water it yourself — it's your horse!" Just like that! The father couldn't make him do it, but the boy had never had much training.

ALLEN QUETONE: Within my own extended family, I have observed how the various children have grown up, and I have often wondered why the parents and grandparents never whipped their kids. I think it comes from respect. The first thing we teach our children is respect for people. The control lies in this respect. As long as kids respect you and therefore listen to you, you don't have to force them to do anything; and you never have to whip them. I have this respect for my father. I would do anything he says. I've never really sat down to figure it out; I just feel that way.

HENRY OLD COYOTE: Children are taught respect even before they start talking. We have a little grandchild, and we try to get her to refrain from touching a person's face. A little child has a tendency to touch your face when you're holding him on your lap. We don't try to discourage our granddaughter, but we try to teach her that it's disrespectful to touch other people's faces.

By having respect for others, you gain respect yourself. If we do something that is not proper, we hear about it from others. We have what we call our 'Teasing Cousins,' who exert an unusual kind of control. They can ridicule us in public — no holds barred.* I have a cousin who is one of the better educated Indians on the Crow reservation, and he and I belong to the same teasing group. If he pulls a boner, I don't let him get away with it. I tease him in public, even though he is one of the better educated Indians of our tribe.

Another form of control that we uphold consists of our relationship to different members of our family and clan. Here again we go back to this question of respect. For instance, I can't pass in front of certain people like the members of my father's clan unless I get permission from them. There is no other way. If these older people of the clan happen to be smoking, I am not supposed to be standing up; I am supposed to sit down until they are through. If any of my clan folk are talking, I don't talk at the same time, even today. I wait until they are through. The same is true of my wife. If she wants to address any of the members of her father's clan and they are smoking, she keeps quiet. But she offers the best she has to these people. She makes them gifts, and in return they make wishes for her. Nowadays you can't get anything unless you pay for it. Money dominates everything in the dominant society. But with the Indian, the value of a gift is determined by the love that goes with it. I am fortunate to have a mother still today who goes out and makes gifts to my clan uncles** on my behalf, because it is my clan uncles who make wishes for me and give me advice as to how to better my life. They are my public relations people. I can't brag myself; it's up to them to brag for me.

JOHN GARDNER: What all of you have just said about respect seems to lie at the center of everything you have expressed during the past several days. It lies at the very center of a person's relation with his fellow man, starting with the child's relation to his family. It lies at the center of man's relation to nature and to the Great Spirit above him. You show that respect is really at the bottom of discipline and authority; it's basic to every kind of learning as well as to the

---

*Cf. Chapter 10, P. 97, for further information on the 'Teasing Cousins.'
**Male members of father's clan. For further information on the members of the father's clan in the Crow tribe, cf. Chapter 10, P. 97.

enjoyment of life. I believe you have used this one word more
than any other single word, and it isn't just a word; it's a
profound attitude.

Nowadays there is very little respect around. Young
people don't especially respect their families; boys do not
respect girls; very few people respect nature; and hardly
anyone bothers to give what lies above much thought, not to
mention respect. So if you have traditions and customs that
lead you by the hand and teach you respect, you're fortunate.
But my impression is that, even among the Indians, many
don't develop as deep a respect as they used to, because as
children they are placed at an early age in the hands of state
schools. Are these schools able to teach loving respect — a
free, not an enforced, kind?

What is it in your traditions that was able to command
respect and work out from it? The reason this is so important
is that white youngsters and white families have pretty well
lost their sense of respect, and insofar as your children get a
white man's education, they too will lose it and are already
losing it. If we want to start improving, instead of further
degenerating, we have to move toward respect, not away from
it.

HENRY OLD COYOTE: I can only speak from
experience. When I was a child I was taught to believe in
something. If you believe in something, you learn to respect
it. Nowadays, most of our younger children no longer know
the proper expressions for the different parts of various
ceremonies. They are not being taught that belief.

In the old days a child was taught to take orders and
follow instructions. Today this is lacking. There are too many
television sets and therefore no time to give and receive this
type of instruction. But in the old days, if a child learned to
take instructions, he would eventually be able to give
instructions. The elders would usually select a child with
leadership qualities on whom they would concentrate their
attention. Like our grandchild. We know she is going to be
some kind of leader. When other children of her age group
come around, she takes over and is boss. You might call it the
leadership qualities in a child showing up at an early age, but

we would like to see her take the lead in something worthwhile, not just be a ringleader!

I know it is part of human nature to see if you can get away with doing something that is forbidden. Back in the old days when they said Indians couldn't have liquor, I used to sneak around to see if I could get some. If you're told not to do something, you want to find out why for yourself. The Indians would meet this tendency head-on by instructing the child and giving him the reasons he shouldn't do certain things. The youngster was held back by principles and reasons.

For example, an older person might tell a child that he would lose a certain amount of respect if he were to do a particular thing. "If you start telling white lies and then go on to big lies, people will recognize you and say, 'Here comes that man who tells lies. Don't listen to him!' And nobody will listen to you from that moment on. If you form a habit of picking things up that don't belong to you, people will say when they see you coming, 'Watch everything! Here comes that man!' If you like to speak your mind any time and anywhere — because this is a free country and you have the right — if you go ahead without respect for others, people will say, 'Here comes that man with a strong tongue and dirty mind. He's coming! Get the women out of here! Get the kids out of here! He's cranky, and we're going to hear some bad words today. A good day is going to end as soon as he comes in. He's going to complain about something; he's going to be cranky about something. Maybe he had it out with his wife and he's going to take it out on us, so get the children and women out of here!' But if you have principles, the doors will always be open. People will be glad to see you and talk to you." These are some of the reasons a grownup might give, to encourage the child not to adopt bad ways.

ALLEN QUETONE: A really small child does what he sees, without knowing; he mimics. He is not called down because he is still too young to be aware of differences. When he reaches a slightly older stage, you point out the differences between things. A boy may be stepping a little bit out of line, or he may be doing something that women do; so he's told,

"We men don't do that. That's woman's work," or "That's a woman's function." Then you give him instructions along the right lines.

VICTOR SARRACINO: It is a known fact that women are the key people in bringing up children. Our women must therefore be treated with extra special care and with kindness and love. Unless we treat them that way, we are going to create a lot of problems within our families. The kids will pick up our behavior because they will see it and assume that that must be the way it's done. How your kids grow up will depend on the way you conduct yourself. Because kids are really good actors. They will do anything you do, not realizing that one way could be wrong and the other way right. So we used to be told that we would be establishing a pattern by our behavior, and leaving a trail and tracks for our children to follow.

One day not too long ago, I was over at Fort Lewis and was invited to attend a workshop on education that was underway. One of the speakers didn't show up and a friend of mine spotted me sitting out there in the audience. He called on me and said, "You're going to be on after the third speaker." I gave this talk, and they printed it. Let me read one or two comments, because it explains briefly how we raise our children. "At home the parents try never to cross their children. If they do and anything happens to the child, such as sickness or an accident, the parents feel it is a punishment for not following the customs that forbid making the child do what he does not want to do. The norm for acting or not acting is "I want to" or "I don't want to," not the rightness or wrongness of the deed. Feeling, not logical reasoning, is what determines performance.

JOHN GARDNER: These are extremely interesting remarks in the context of our present culture. Many modern parents let their children do what they want to do, but the results are not good. You feel, however, that what you're talking about works out well, and is in line with old traditions. All of you have emphasized that the child should be obedient, should be respectful. Now you are saying that you should never cross the child. Does that mean never? What if the parent says, "I want you to do this; would you please do this?" and the child says, "I don't want to!" like the boy whose father asked him to water the horse?

VICTOR SARRACINO: It means only until the child begins to reason. As soon as the child is old enough, you can explain *why* it would be unwise to do certain things. If the child has had proper discipline, he or she will automatically do what you ask, whether or not there is any logic to it. It will just be automatic. That's the whole point. I feel that I have never been commanded to do anything. I have been asked, but I automatically do it. But the parents have to set the example. I remember that my mother used to say to me, "Whenever you tell your child to do something, make sure that you go through with it yourself. Go through with it and never try to cross your children by disobeying your own advice. If you do, they will follow your bad example in future years." In other words, I shouldn't tell them not to drink alcoholic beverages because it will harm them, and turn around and drink alcohol myself. Whatever I tell them to do, I must be sure to do myself.

JOHN GARDNER: I believe that what you have just said contains the crux of true discipline, which in turn brings safety and strength to a child. You said that the child is a marvelous actor. He does what we *do*, not what we *say to do*. So we must be careful how we act. That is your first principle, applying to the very young child. Your second principle is: if parents are respected and they say, "I would like you to do this," their child will do it automatically, because they have real authority. Later, when the child comes to the stage of reason, he can begin to see the principles on which things are based. He begins to develop independent judgment. But first he has put down roots in the example and loving authority of his parents. Unfortunately, these steps are no longer clear to most people. Parents today are pretty mixed up on the subject of authority and discipline.

The priorities in the traditional Indian way and in our modern way are exactly reversed. Let me explain what I mean. A man has a will with which he does things; he has a heart with which he feels, and he has a head with which he thinks. If you were to locate his will somewhere, you would put it down in the lower body, in the legs and feet, in the active, moving part of him. You would locate his feelings in his breast and heart, and you would put his thinking up in his head. I believe the Indian starts his education with the will. The child imitates whatever his elders do. First the feet walk in a certain manner, then the feeling arises, then the thinking comes clear about the previous deeds and feelings.

In the ordinary white man's education, it's exactly the opposite. Everything aims at the head right from the beginning. It's head, head, head, all the time. As to feeling, it doesn't seem to mean much; and where will is concerned, most of our educators think that if you've got something straight in your head, you can perform it correctly. That's what they think and hope.

ALLEN QUETONE: It's interesting that our grand-parents never used to punish us kids. In our tribe, and the same was true of other tribes, you didn't whip children. As Victor said, you taught them mainly by example. The grandparents and parents lived according to the values and principles they wanted children to respect. In addition, because of the conditions in which the Plains Tribes lived, a boy had to possess certain other qualities. He had to possess spirit — not in the sense in which we've been using the word, but in the sense of 'spirit of the individual' — the vigor, the drive, the energy that an individual has and that makes for warriors. In this regard, the child was not restricted; he was encouraged to develop these traits. When he reached maturity, you had an individual who on the one hand tried to embody the best character traits, and on the other hand, if roused to anger, had a very free spirit that was unrestrained. This spirit was nurtured as part of a child's early training, but in such a way that it came out only in time of need. I guess it came out when a person's survival was at stake, and then there was no stopping it.

MAX HANLEY: My grandfathers, my grandmothers and my mother hardly ever spanked at all. My grandfather said that if you spanked the little ones, you made them scared and they couldn't think. My great great-grandfathers used to use the double rope, but they never hit you; they would just barely miss you with that rope. Afterwards, they would go easy, easy. They would take this boy or girl and talk very softly and kindly to them, and these youngsters would listen.

As soon as the baby started walking and started saying a few things, the parents and grandparents would teach it what to do and what not to do. The mama would tell it not to do this because something would happen to it; when the little baby started walking, she would try to scare it so as to keep it from certain things, especially the fire. Sometimes at night you would hear the owl. So they made the baby listen to the owl right into the darkness. And when the baby started crying, maybe at table, the mother or father would say, "Baby, be quiet; the owl will hear you." In my days I used to hear wolves. We were living close to the mountains where there are some canyons. In the evening after the sun went down, I could hear the wolf make a long howl. I could hear the echo in the canyon. So let the little children hear the cry of the wolf as it goes into the woods somewhere; then when they get mad about something or try to do something unusual, you can say, "The owl or the wolf will do this or that to you, so you mustn't cry." Then the child will stop.

ALLEN QUETONE: There were many ways by which the Indians kept their young people in line or made them aware of what they had to do. Much of this was in terms of taboos and fears. In other words, we have all kinds of stories and legends about how if you do this, this will happen to you, or if you do that — such as eating or drinking something you're not supposed to eat or drink — something else will happen to you. This training started right at birth. It was effective, so the need for corporal punishment was at a minimum. The tribes used a great deal of scolding and a great deal of scaring. It worked, and each generation went through this conditioning. Today, this is no longer done. The things that you and I experienced are not practiced at all any more.

ARTHUR SUTTON: To my way of thinking, every child has to have a starting point. My starting point was obedience to the person who reared me. If I hadn't had obedience, I wouldn't have known how to obey the laws that were

presented to me while I was growing up. For instance, my
grandmother who raised me would say, "This is you. What
I'm saying is going to grow around you. My words must take
root, in order for you to go on and live by them. You must
try to practice what I am teaching you, if you want to get
along in the world. What I am telling you is going to come
out one at a time. Therefore, when you get face to face with
problems, you're going to understand what I'm driving at.
When these obstacles come along, you won't have any
difficulty solving them."

I patterned my life as best I could according to her
philosophy and teachings. That's one reason I was chosen to
be a tribal leader. It was because I took the advice of the
older elements that was teaching me. I had another way to go
if I had been so inclined, my white way; but no, I stuck to
my poor Indian grandmother who raised me. I took her
words, and her words still stick with me today. This is what
she said, "Do unto others as you would have them do unto
you." In other words, look to the people. If they need help,
render your services.

My mother died when I was young, so it was my
grandmother who gave me advice. Then when I got a little
older, my grandfather stepped in. He taught me how to
approach different people and he said, "My friend, when men

are talking together, never come
around and disturb them. Go off
somewhere and play until I call
you." That's one of the strict pieces
of advice I got from him and I
abided by it. When the older men
got together and talked things over,
we children went off somewhere
and left them to themselves. We
didn't butt in like the younger
generation does today. Youngsters
today run over everything because
they've never had the proper kind

ARTHUR SUTTON —   of teaching. Nowadays the parents
Arapaho

talk about all sorts of things at the dinner table and the kids are all ears. "If my parents can do these things, why can't I?" That's what they say. But it was different with me. My grandparents were careful not to talk about certain things in front of me, and if I started talking, they would say, "Now you keep quiet. We didn't ask you to butt in." So I just kept quiet.

I try to look out for the younger element today and teach them things that will be helpful in their lives. This is the way they reply: "You live your life; let us live ours." My answer is, "If your friends can give you better advice than I'm giving you, then take it. But when your friends will have nothing more to do with you, who will you fall back on? You're going to fall right back on me for advice." There are several who have already done that. When they get into trouble, when they need help, to whom do they go? To poor me. I was always brought up to believe that in the long run accepting advice does more good than harm. And it saves a lot of grief.

I don't know how many times we got a licking when we disobeyed orders as kids. For instance, in 1936 we went to Arkansas to visit my dad. He was a white man. A half brother of mine was sitting on a singletree and my father was fixing a doubletree. "Son," he says, "Get that singletree you're sitting on." My brother, who thought he was smart, said, "You get it yourself." The old man disconnects the other singletree and hits him with it. He says, "Now bring it to me. I'm the boss as long as you still put your feet under my table. If you don't like the way I'm boss, see that road over there? You can hit it if you think you're so smart." I just sat there and looked at my dad. He turned to me and said, "And you, young man, do you want the same treatment?" I told him I hadn't said anything, that I was just looking at him. So he told me, "Well then, you got different training from these boys. Their mother is sticking up for them; that's the reason they're in such bad shape. But you're different. I know the old lady who raised you. She was strict. You had good training. I'm not scared of your going into the world. I know you'll make it."

JOHN GARDNER: As you've just observed, parents today don't bring up their children the way you were raised. This is how they reason it out for themselves. "I want my boy to grow up to be a leader. I want him to be independent in his judgment and I want him to be informed. These are the objectives at which I am aiming. To train him properly, therefore, I will inform him all the time; I will reason with him and explain everything to him and bring him in on all my conversations. I don't want to teach my little child to be obedient, because that would make him a follower. I want him to be a leader; therefore, he shouldn't be obedient.

The fact that parents don't 'force' their children to do things is fundamentally a different thing from the Indian practice of refraining from force and demands. Unlike the Indians, white parents today fail to instill in their children a respect for others and a respect for what is greater than they. As a result, their children tend to follow only their own inclinations. As a further result, the children are both confused and unhappy.

ARTHUR SUTTON: If you take a seed and set it in the ground, you're going to have to nurture it for it to grow into a healthy plant. Now, an Indian puts advice in a young child's ear, and that child usually listens because of his respect and the training he has had. An Indian who listens gets somewhere. A person who does not listen gets nowhere, like my cousin. He used to run down to the river and take a bath every morning without eating breakfast. The old lady got tired of it. One day she said to her next door neighbor. "My grandson doesn't mind me. Could you do something about it?" Her neighbor goes down to the river and gets the young man and says, "Son, you get over there and mind your grandmother. If you don't, I'm going to get you." So my cousin comes back and takes a few bites of breakfast. He listens to see if that man has walked away, then out he goes. But that man was standing back there with a shotgun. He sees that boy run, so he shouts, "Hey, you! Stop!" That boy turns and says, "Stop me!" The gun goes off over his head, so my cousin stops in his tracks. That's the way some children who don't listen have to learn.

JOHN GARDNER: I am thinking of the fact that you, Arthur, are now a leader, and that you said you took your starting point from obedience. Apparently, obedience didn't prevent you from becoming a leader. On the contrary, it helped you; but a lot of parents can't see that.

ARTHUR SUTTON: A lot of the younger element don't see that either. They are just turned loose and do as they please. They say, "Well, I'm my own boss. I can do what I want." That's what is ruining our nation today.

JOHN GARDNER: I believe the loss of discipline has to do with our modern ideas of what leadership consists of. Somebody at lunch was asking Arthur how you get to be a leader and a chief. I was listening from several seats down and heard him say that you are inspected, you are looked over for quite some time to see if you are worthy. Many people nowadays have the idea that a leader is the man who can throw his personal weight around most impressively, and that this makes him chief. From everything Arthur has said, he didn't stop being obedient when he stopped being a child. In fact, he is probably a leader today because people feel that he is still most obedient, not to parents, of course, but to what is right and best. Obedience, therefore, is a direct line of training to leadership. This is how I interpret it. As a child, you are obedient to your elders; as an adult, you are obedient to ideals. Moreover, if you don't *really* believe there is something higher than yourself as an adult, you will lose your authority with the young.

HENRY OLD COYOTE: I am sorry for many of the things I did as a youngster and many of the stunts I pulled, and I am trying to make up for them in various ways. But I had to believe in something in order to control myself. That's what they mean, I guess, when they tell the child to believe. Whether you believe in the white man's religion or the Indian way, believe in something and believe in yourself. The Indians don't force anybody to do anything; they tell you the good points and it's up to you to volunteer. Nobody ever forced me to go out and fast or participate in any ceremony. I did it because I wanted to. They made me feel I should, but they didn't force me. The Indians stress the fact that you should believe in something, because if you believe in a principle, you are able to guide yourself toward that principle.

8
ADOLESCENCE—
A NEW PHASE

JOHN GARDNER: The two great periods of a child's early life are when he is first brought into the world and still lives in the innocence of childhood, and adolescence, when all of the impurity occurs. Today in particular, many kinds of twists take place at adolescence, because we can't find the right ways to deal with this period in a child's life. The fact that we fail undermines the future life of the adolescent — his marriage, parenthood and so on, which in turn undermines the next generation. So our culture gets off to a very bad start unless the matter of adolescence is handled well. Since there is so much today that goes wrong during this phase of life, and because so much degeneracy is setting in, we would be grateful to hear some of the Indians' traditional ideas about how the girl and the boy should develop in the finest way through adolescence and courtship to marriage. What is the traditional ideal?

HENRY OLD COYOTE: At about that age of adolescence, my grandfather used to tell me, "It's all right to have friends, but these friends will have some influence on you and you will tend to forget the good instructions and good advice you had. By trying to make you feel like a man, they'll get you to do something that you know isn't right, like daring you to chew tobacco, or daring you to smoke in school to see if you can get away with it, or going out and pulling some tricks on your neighbors." I took my first drink of alcohol on a dare from one of my friends. He told me, "You're not man enough!" but I showed him that I was.

The ones who exerted the strongest influence were usually those from broken homes who went from place to place and were much more on their own than the rest. They didn't care what they did, because no one was contributing to their livelihood. They were on their own, so they did as they pleased. They, and the ones who followed them, wanted to be modern, so they broke their ties. They're the ones who got us to do things, and we had to go along with them to belong to the group. In order to be 'in,' we had to do the things they did, although deep inside we knew it was wrong.

I knew one boy, same age as I, who had good schooling, but he lost his people while quite young. Today with that good schooling, he's an alcoholic. He's severed all ties with his own people. He still has relatives living on the reservation, but he doesn't want to come too far in, so he stays right on the outskirts in one of the towns adjoining the reservation. We still see him, we know who he is; but he's gone his own way and severed all ties. All the things that I was told and observed, he also knew as a boy. His grandfather was living and I know he got the same instructions that I had when I was growing up, but after his grandfather died, he went away to school. When he came back he used to chide us for not wearing the same clothes he did, because he was modern while we still rode horseback and wore boots. "What's the matter?" he would say; "You're acting like cowboys. Want to be cowboys and Indians?" and things like that. He's modern and prefers modern music to Indian music. He influenced a lot of boys in my own group. Because he didn't believe these things himself, he used to tell us, "Some of the things you're doing are just based on superstition. You should go drinking, instead. Have a good time! Forget about your troubles!"

The same thing happens with teenagers today. In order to be 'in' with a certain group, they do the things the others are doing. Merely by listening and following the suggestions of others, some of these kids who have been taught to respect the word have forgotten that respect. When they go to high school, they're exposed to another thinking, which is different from the thinking they got from their grandparents. Like one of the Crow boys who went out to the West Coast and came back and introduced gas inhaling and glue sniffing and now has introduced marihuana. I understand he can reach into any of his pockets and come up with an LSD tablet. People like that have an influence on others. In my own case, I knew it was wrong; but I went along with some of my buddies' suggestions in order to be 'in' with them, when I should have been out tending to something more useful. We'd get in the car and see how fast we could go, see how fast we could turn a corner and things like that; daring each other in a way that was different from the darings of our elders who challenged us not to hesitate to take a plunge into ice-cold water, or to stay inside a sweat lodge no matter how hot it became Our elders were intent on teaching us to control our bodies, and to gain patience by being able to force ourselves to stand it.

I myself was a spoiled child. Being the eldest of the boys, I more or less had my way if I wanted to enjoy myself. Someday I would realize what I was doing and would use it to advise my nephews and brothers, but I had to learn the hard way. I had broken bones in just about every limb by not showing good judgment. And I was pretty free to do what I wanted, like enjoying good horses or something like that, because freedom is part of the Indian's early training — freedom of the child and freedom of the parent. If my parents had food, I enjoyed this food; but then they made me realize that they were free to enjoy their lives, too, and that I couldn't be on their hands all the time. If I was to contribute anything to my parents while they were living, I was reminded of that. The way they put it to me was that it was not an obligation. They didn't force me to do it; they made me feel it was right to do it, and I wanted to do it because of the training I had had. In fact, I would have felt guilty for not doing it.

SYLVESTER MOREY: Do any of the young Indians go out and fast nowadays? That is a form of adolescence training that is completely unknown to the whites.

HENRY OLD COYOTE: Yes. In fact, my nephew, who is only about 15, wanted to go and fast last summer. I encouraged him, and so, I being the only sponsor he had, he came to me. I advised him and told him what he should and should not do while he was out there and that he should not run away from something he starts.

Afterwards my nephew felt he had really accomplished something and won something for himself. He came back and thanked me for making him think that way. I didn't tell him to do it, but I encouraged him. So today, if he has a dollar to spare, he buys me tobacco or something to eat. And he always has a greeting, a kind word for me. He realizes there is something greater than he, and I believe that's what has helped him along with his studies. I told him that he should always ask for assistance from that greater force. So he's got that idea, and he's certainly a more successful Indian. Just last week he got his high school diploma, so he wrote me a thank-you note.

Since you also wanted to hear about the training girls go through, I'll cover that briefly. To give you an example: Stella, my wife, lost her mother when she was quite young, but she was adopted by another woman. Her aunt was there, too, so she got a lot of information from both of them. You might say that these two people were responsible for what she is and for the respect that she has.

They stressed what is desirable in a woman. She was taught how to be a good housekeeper, and that she should follow certain rituals in preparing food, like filling herself with a certain feeling before going out to pick berries or roots. She was told that she should be kind to others and that, even though she might feel like slapping a man, she should talk to him nicely. She was given the background on how these things came about and was taught to have respect for the home. She was also told what thoughts go into the different parts of the clothing she might make. Stella is noted for her beadwork and her patterns and for preparing hides. In fact, I believe she and her sister-in-law are the only Indians so far to take any prizes from the Woodlawn Exhibit at Mt.

STELLA and HENRY OLD COYOTE — Crow

Vernon, which is a nationwide exhibit. She's pretty modest about it. She doesn't brag, because by her training its unbecoming to brag. You can acknowledge praise, but never brag.

Here's one example of what a man looks for in a woman. There was a good man, a wise man, who was looking for a wife for his son. He said, "I'm going to find a wife for you." So he sat on a little hill and had a bunch of little pebbles there, and asked the girls to ride by during the moving of the camp. The caravan was right below him, so he'd throw these little pebbles and hit the horse and the horse would jump and these little girls would turn around and really bawl him out in no uncertain terms. One girl happened to pass under him. He threw that pebble and by luck he hit her right on the head. She just stopped. She never looked; she just stopped, then kept going. He said, "Son, that's your wife."

JOHN GARDNER: When we talk about adolescence, what actually is it? It's the time of sexual maturity. Today, young people are being taught that sex is a natural thing. They understand natural in the sense that it's natural like eating, and a person eats more or less when and what he pleases. So young people are being taught that they should feel free and easy about the expression of sex, and this means that they become promiscuous. All of this is considered natural. It is said that the Puritans or the Victorians were the ones who put all kinds of taboos on sex and that if we didn't have the hangups that resulted, we would all be free; there would be plenty of relationships between boys and girls before marriage and after marriage, too.

Now the Indian represents someone who lives close to nature; he had reverence for nature and took his lessons from nature. If the Indian speaks more to the real condition of nature, what does he say about this? I have heard that there are Indian traditions that match the older religious traditions of white cultures, to the effect that whether a person is promiscuous or chaste will affect the development of his spiritual life. The whole question of purity and chastity is very important to young people. They need to know what the ideal is. I have heard that Indian warriors, as well as a person who was to become a medicine man, had to take these things into special account.

HENRY OLD COYOTE: The virtue of purity was highly valued. The virtues they look for in a man and in a woman come out in the instructions we have been talking about. Some of these things were discussed frankly between mother and daughter, and between father and son. They were a part of our life until the Christians, the white man do-gooders, came into contact with the Indians and these facts of life turned out to be vulgar. They couldn't even speak about them any longer.

Among the Indians, a virtuous woman is to be desired. A virtuous woman plays a prominent part in some of the ceremonies we have. White people have a tendency to interpret things through the values of their own culture. So when we look for a virtuous woman to perform certain services in some of the ceremonies, the white man thinks of the Virgin Mary, Christ's mother, but this interpretation is away from the original intent of the ceremony. That's why the Indian is often reluctant to give the full picture of the role the woman plays in certain ceremonies.

Because of her respect for purity, there are certain things a woman will refrain from saying at certain times. And at certain times of the month, during the menstruation period, the woman doesn't stay inside the tipi. She doesn't want to be in the presence of the medicine bundle; she doesn't want to be in the tipi because of the symbols it represents. You might say that it is a time when the woman feels unclean, so she leaves the household and lives in a little shelter all by herself until that period ends. Even today, if it happens to be that time of month, a woman won't go near a ceremony, though the inner self is anxious to go. Or if she happens to be part of the ceremony, she admits that that period has come. Then they make incense and bless all the rest of the people and allow the woman to go home so that she will be away from there. That respect is instilled in the young lady from the time she has her first period until what you might call the change of life. When that time comes, the woman feels free to be a participant in the ceremonies at all times.

This respect that we talk about, however, has been shattered by non-Indians. For instance, I have had the experience of seeing non-Indian teenagers out at Lake Mead near Las Vegas. While the parents are over there gambling, the children have all that beach to themselves, where they practice sex openly in broad daylight, with people going back and forth. When Indian teenagers see that, they think, "If the white people can do that, so can we." Also, when the women got together in the old days, they freely discussed the problems they might encounter as a woman: pregnancy, parenthood, and all that; but that information is lacking today. Some of the things they watched for and tried to avoid are being ignored because of the simple fact that the white man has introduced scientific methods, and it wouldn't be practical to go back to old grandmother's tales.

So what can you do? The traditional Indian, who has other morals to present for the benefit of his children, is undermined. You might say it's a barrier created by the white people that those who are in a position to give that traditional advice or instruction are barred from the classrooms. So young Indians are cut off from a deeper understanding of the traditional virtues when they are away at school. They practice in the modern world. Even though the traditional Indian education is good for Indian children, they have a tendency to look at their people's ways of respect as primitive.

9
THE ROLE OF
THE GRANDPARENTS

ALLEN QUETONE: The grandmother plays a very important role in teaching and forming the values of children and in trying to rear them in accordance with tribal and family standards. She performs many of the duties for which the parents don't have time. My grandmother was the daughter of a chief. My oldest sister and one of my first cousins were fortunate enough to have been exposed to her influence and what she did for them is really something. She died before the rest of us in the family were old enough to come under her influence. But she gave my sister and cousin, two women, the real old Kiowa training and they were greatly affected by it — they still possess the traits and qualities that come from that old Kiowa upbringing. I was exposed to this training, but not nearly as much as I would like to have been.

The point is, my grandmother was of a family that would settle only for the very best. In the Kiowa tribe, and I'm sure this is true of other tribes, a family has a certain standard to maintain by raising its children in a certain manner. We call this "aw day," meaning that you heap the very best on your children — the best treatment, the best training, the best of everything. You don't overwork them; you don't let anything happen to them. You raise them like queen bees. The paradoxical thing is that by your doing this, the children develop qualities that are great and good on the one hand, and on the other hand they develop the strength and character that enable them to survive under the worst of circumstances. Unfortunately, not everybody is raised this way nowadays.

HENRY OLD COYOTE: The feeling of grandparents for their grandchildren can be expressed this way: "Our children are dear to us; but when we have grandchildren, they seem to be more dear than our children were." You might say that the grandmother falls all over herself to try to show her appreciation for her grandchild. It goes right back to those wishes that were made for them when they were little girls: the wish that they would live to become grandmothers someday. So when the time comes and they reach grandmotherhood, they do extra little duties to show their appreciation.

I was practically raised by my grandparents. Although my parents were living, they were out traveling all over the country, and so I stayed with my grandfolks. My grandmother used to sing lullabies to me, and she used to tell me those stories about little animals and so forth. Then, after I grew older, my grandfather started telling me stories that deal with what people expect in a man and with the facts of life, such as what the different parts of the cradle represent, what the significance of the tipi is, how it came into existence, and why it faces east. After I had heard the story of the tipi, my grandmother took me out and showed me how to put it up. I've never made a mistake in putting up a tipi, or forgotten how since that first time, because I had been told what each pole and each part stands for and in what sequence they go; in other words, because I had been given all the necessary background.

What I had been told might be called stories and legends, but they are full of information. This information is passed on to the person who is likely to pass it on for the benefit of others. So since I was the eldest of the boys, my grandfather told me these stories relating how the various customs and traditions originated, and it is up to me to try and remember all these things in order to pass the right information on to the people who are next in line or to the person who is receptive to that remembering. This is what I picked up from my grandparents. I might say that I was very fortunate in coming into contact with them.

ARTHUR SUTTON: I, myself, didn't have any man to teach me until I was about nine or ten years of age. As I've told you, I was reared by my grandmother. She seldom explained what the man's side would be. What she said was this, "I'm going to tell you the way I raised you after you were born. I took you away from your mother when she died, because I wanted to raise you according to what I knew." From then on I listened to her. She used to tell me, "Now listen here, young man. When you get old, what I'm teaching you is going to come back to you, so you'd better listen good and put down in your memory what I'm telling you so that you never forget it." I followed her advice.

Later on, when my Cheyenne grandfather began to teach me all sorts of things, he said, "Young man, if you want to be a man, don't lie in bed till noon." I said, "Why?" He said, "Your blood will get so still that you'll be lazy. You have to get up early to do the things that a man should do in later years." So he started teaching me. Still later, my brother stepped in and told me all he knew. They are the only people who taught me different things.

But I lay all the credit to my old grandmother for the shape I'm in today. If I hadn't heeded her teachings and her warnings, I don't think I would be in the position I am in now. I'd be like some of those poor young men and women who are on the street today pulling that cork and dumping it on. That's a sickness, they claim. My grandmother used to say, "You're going to get to the place where you will see how this alcohol works. You may take and use this alcohol," she said, "because the road is wide, the road has plenty of alcohol and many different things that will mislead you. But if you take my advice and live the best way you can without using this stuff, you're going to go a long way and your health will be better in the long run." But I was too smart; I started using alcohol. Now, those words of my grandmother came back to me when I was lying on my deathbed. Alcohol caused my trouble as well as smoking, which went together with it. So I was a 'smart' man to use those things, but not as smart as the old lady was. I thought I was smart, but I wasn't.

MAX HANLEY: I was raised by my grandmother and also by my grandfather. I have three grandfathers in all and two grandmothers. When I was a little boy around five, six and seven years old, there used to be some kind of ceremonials at my grandmother's place. These other people, our neighbors who lived a mile or two away, all came; and when they got through the ceremony in the evening, they started talking to each other about what happened in the past. I was small and I wasn't supposed to be listening. I was supposed to be asleep because I had to look after the sheep the next day; otherwise, I might fall asleep somewhere and the sheep would stray away. So I pretended to be sleeping. I just closed my eyes and listened until way late at night. They told jokes and funny stories just like we did last night, and I enjoyed myself until I began to get sleepy.

I was raised by my grandmother and my older sister. My grandmother always told us what to do about the livestock. We used to have about 12 cows. One of my uncles looked after these few cows and another uncle took care of the horses. So when my uncles came back in the evening, they told us where they had been and what had happened during the day — how they had caught a horse or herded some cattle. Also, how they had gotten down into a canyon with their rope and what you're supposed to do when you're in that canyon — how you hold on, how you must be sure to tie the rope to a rock or tree so that you won't fall off. They were always telling us about such things and I really enjoyed myself.

My mother and father were always busy. My mother used to be weaving, carding and spinning; my father was always traveling someplace. He was a medicine man, by the way. Somebody was always coming to get him to do the Blessing Way or what they call the Hand Trembler, and so he would travel four or five or maybe ten miles. Suppose a patient was sick and nobody knew what was ailing him or her. My father would do the Hand Trembler. He would wash his hands, roll up his sleeves, and take corn pollen and sprinkle it on a particular place. Then he would pray a special prayer. After he made the short prayer, he would sing; and while he was still singing he would start moving his right hand a little here and there. All this time he had his eyes closed and was thinking. Then he made all kinds of motions, and the patient had to guess what these motions were all about. The patient had to try to remember anything that had happened to him in the past — like maybe he stepped on a snake — because there might be two or three things causing the sickness. Sometimes he would guess pretty quickly, and then the hand would just drop. Then the medicine man would rub his hand because it had gotten numb and he didn't feel anything in it. You know what it feels like when you touch an electric cord and get a shock? It's just like that. Anyway, that's the kind of thing my father did when he stayed away for two and three days.

When I was at home and my mother and father were there, they didn't say much to me. They were always too busy doing something. So I didn't enjoy myself over there. But I liked to stay with my grandmother. She always had something to tell me and my sister, too. She used to tell us this and that and all kinds of stories, so we liked to stay with grandmother all the time. It seems as if these days the mother and father are always too busy; they don't have enough time to talk to the children.

JOHN GARDNER: Every person here has said the same thing about his grandparents. You all had different kinds of grandparents, but every single one of you was grateful for having gotten your main inspiration and main guidance from them. Is this still true today? For example, if I read the white world correctly, the attitude you have expressed toward your grandparents is not very true of us. With us, the very first thing that happens when you get married is that you get into trouble with your mother-in-law. That's the very first thing. Then you have two choices: you can either submit to her, or you can get out or push her out — one or the other. It's so radically different from what you describe. I've seen a few families where the grandparents are very much honored and most welcome. But I have noticed even more frequently that grandparents are not much honored and are not even very welcome. In many young people's minds, they are difficult people to get along with; therefore, this extraordinarily beneficial relationship that you have described, which is good for the old and good for the young, often doesn't occur.

Why is it that older people are not held in such high esteem in our present-day culture? I don't think the Indians have any old people's home where you send hundreds of old people to live, but white people have all sorts of retirement communities scattered over the country where old people go and where they have nothing to do with their families. They have no teaching position, they are not telling stories, they are not setting any example or giving out any wisdom. They aren't doing any of these things because if they lived at home with their children and grandchildren, there would inevitably be come kind of disturbance.

I have often thought how strange it is that parents have children before they have much life experience; so they must bring up their children without life experience. This grandparent arrangement that the Indians had seems so wise to me because if old people have a good attitude, they also have enough experience at least to have something really to say.

ALLEN QUETONE: I would say two things. Just two days before coming here, my sisters told me that we ought to have an early Father's Day celebration for my father. So we had a little get-together for him. I have two small sons, seven and nine, and they unfortunately have been reared like any of your kids. We've travelled around the country and they haven't been exposed to Indian ways, except through me, of course. I noticed that my father had one of the boys on his lap and was talking to him. Pretty soon he went to the car where he had a bow and arrow for each boy; then he came back and sat down with them and was talking with them some more. When we were on our way home, I asked the boys what their grandfather had said. They said that he had told them the bows and arrows were for them to play with and that they were supposed to learn how to use them, but

ALLEN QUETONE —
Kiowa (Conference Chairman)

not to hurt anybody with them. They were for shooting at things in play, but not for shooting at people or domestic animals. Here is an example of doing things in the present day and age that were done in the past; because, as somebody here observed, kids mimic older people as they go through the various stages of their growth. Young kids, at least in the Plains tribes — and I say this for the benefit of the Eastern Seaboard and the Southwest tribes — were taught how to handle the bow and arrow; they played at war games and fighting and rode stick horses and real horses.

So my first point is that being raised by our grandparents couldn't have been a happier time. Having this contact with them meant a great deal. I wouldn't have had the opportunity or fun of growing as a boy with my father as I had with my grandfather. As I recall, my father didn't have time to stay in any one place for long; he was constantly moving. I, on the other hand, had a leisurely upbringing and was very much influenced by my grandparents, though I wish I had been even more influenced by them in terms of the knowledge and wisdom I now know they possessed.

The other point is that old people under the old way had a philosophy of being a kind of excess baggage, and so they weren't too demanding. I don't know how it is in the present day because I haven't been around old people very much in the last 10 or 15 years. But I do remember that the older people were reconciled to not having too much attention paid them and not being a burden, mainly because of the necessity for almost constant and quick movement. And yet they had a very strong influence. At least this was true of the Plains tribes.

ARTHUR SUTTON: Let me put it another way. Present-day parents use these grandparents as babysitters. The parents turn their kids over to the grandparents for better training and forget about them, so that they can go off and do as they please. If they don't have any grandparents on either side, they just turn them loose and tell them, "Go mind your own business while we have our own fun right here." That's where a lot of the trouble starts.

ERNEST BENEDICT: In my own case, I lived with my grandmother for a period of five years. Soon after that, she came and lived with us until she died. So at least as I was growing up, my grandmother — my mother's mother — was very important to the family. We did visit my father's mother once in a while, but not very often.

This situation is the same today. My wife's mother and father both died before we got married. Since then my mother, who is still alive, has been standing in as the mother of my wife. The children address her as 'Grandmother,' and she is very much a part of their lives. She has a house close to where we live, and the children play at either place. In effect, we live together — one home with two dwellings. But the grandmother, my mother, is an essential part of our household and gives very strict orders.

MAX HANLEY: I have 12 grandchildren. They wanted to come to our place every weekend from Window Rock, but it's 162 miles away. So once a month they like to visit us. The reason they like to come to grandmother's is that my wife is always giving them money. She also makes tortillas and fried bread and hominy stew and all that good Indian food. That's what draws them to our place all the time.

My oldest grandson's name is Mike Hanley. Last year he killed a two pointer deer, and he wanted to know how to skin it the Indian way. He and three other boys came, and I showed them how to cut. If you're taking the whole skin off, you have to cut all the way down, then skin the head. I guess you know there is a hollow place right in the eye. You have to be very careful to cut right under this hollow and take everything out, even the eyebrow; then you cut all the way to the horn. After that you take out everything that's inside — what we call the guts, and so forth. So Mike and the boys had that experience and learned. The second time they went hunting, one of them killed another deer. Mike and the three others cut it open exactly the way I had shown them, even though I wasn't there — at least, that's what my son, Wallace Hanley, told me.

That's where education comes in. With the Navajos, the grandparents still do a lot to teach the little ones these things, also how to handle guns and bows and arrows, and where to hit. They learn quite a bit, these young children. I know that's the way I learned, especially about Navajo culture, before I went to school.

VICTOR SARRACINO: I know that many times children get really attached to their grandparents, and the grandparents don't seem to mind at all. Sometimes they take in the little ones, not just for the summer but all year round. This is different from what you mentioned in the dominant society, where the old folks are left alone.

With us it's a different situation altogether, even today. For example, before I left to come here, my wife's grandmother came from another village the day before Father's Day to have a celebration because I wouldn't be there on the day itself. Then my eldest daughter went after my mother, who lives about two blocks away from us. Now, I have my mother-in-law living with us — she used to live by herself and she just decided to move in, which is fine. Then another one of my kids said, "Why don't we go to our other great-grandmother's?" She lives about two blocks from us in the opposite direction from my own mother, and every Friday my wife goes after this other grandmother of hers. So we had four grandmothers right there, or to be more exact, two grandmothers and two great-grandmothers. We've always thought we should just take all of them in and have them live with us. This way our kids could learn something from them. That's what we're working toward, little by little. We don't want to rush them in, but we're bringing them in little by little, because we have a place big enough to keep them all. Last night I talked to my wife on the phone, and she had three of them with her; so it's beginning to work. The kids love it and want to talk to them all the time.

ARTHUR SUTTON: I want to relate this to you. When

we left Oklahoma City, my grandmother went after her great-grandkids, to be the babysitter. That's how much she loved her grandchildren — she flew to Oklahoma to go after her grandchildren and bring them back to Washington, D.C. to take care of them. If she hadn't any love for her grandchildren, she would have left them where they were. But she had so much love for them that she flew all that distance and brought them back. I saw it with my own eyes.

You see, a grandmother doesn't have her own children to mess with any longer. She feels lost, because she's been a mother for so many years. She wants to take care of someone again, so she falls back on her grandchildren; she can be a mother to these kids. In my case, my mother-in-law died, so we had to do the best we could with our kids. Now we ourselves have grandchildren, so we're the ones who have to beg those grandchildren to come and stay with us so that we can give them the training they should have.

JOHN GARDNER: I may be a little cynical about this; but I have often noticed that some grandparents love their grandchildren very much — they are their own flesh and blood, and they're proud of that — but they don't always have too good an influence on them. They frequently indulge and spoil them, and so exploit them for their own satisfaction.

ALLEN QUETONE: I believe there is a slight difference between this and the way Indians treat their grandchildren. On the one hand, Indians can be overly protective, and there's probably a selfish satisfaction on the part of grandparents in giving kids their utmost. On the other hand, they also go to the other extreme of being strictly formalized and trying to rear their grandchildren in a disciplined manner. So a certain balance is maintained.

As a new recruit to the dominant system, I can see why the white man, even if he wanted to, could not possibly have the time under this system to provide the care and teaching to his grandchildren that the Indians give. I know the way my grandfather treated me, and though I don't have grandchildren yet, I know what I would want them to be exposed to. But I would never have the time to pay as much attention to them as my grandfather paid to me, if I intended to keep up with the system. So what I'm going to do when I reach a certain stage is quit. I'm not going to fight it the way the non-Indians do. They're on a treadmill; and they know it, but they can't stop. I see no good reason why a man should work so hard right into his old age. This is one of the differences between the total Indian philosophy as opposed to the non-Indian philosophy that we are trying to define at this conference.

JOHN GARDNER: I believe the cause for working too hard too long is the same as what compels most of us to travel faster all the time. There is a control here that we don't teach in our culture. We don't teach a man how to arrive. To hurry on, yes; to arrive fully and enjoy life, no. Since people never sufficiently enjoy the things they have in hand, they have to keep moving. Then when they retire, many people are likely to fall apart, because the only thing that kept them in one piece, which was the routine of rushing, is gone. So many men postpone retirement as long as possible. Since they don't seem to have any really deep enjoyment of nature and many don't enjoy people outside their own family, which may nevertheless reject them, they prefer to stay with the treadmill, going faster and faster to make up for the fact that they are not really ever going to arrive. Here we have another reason why we are talking together. The problems of age have their roots in early education.

10
FAMILY AND
CLAN STRUCTURE

HENRY OLD COYOTE: Our people are divided into clans. Originally we had 13 clans, but now we're down to about 9, because some of the clans have been absorbed into others. In our clan system we automatically belong to the mother's clan and are identified with that clan. I happen to belong to what is known as the Whistling Water Clan and my wife belongs to the Greasy Mouths. The original name for my clan was Prairie Dog Do-Gooders, but someone in our clan married back into his own clan. So then there was a joke about it, that these people who married back into their own clan would go along the waterways whistling. That's why they gave us the name, 'Whistling Waters.' My wife's clan were noted for getting good game. They had greasy mouths all the time and because of it, got that name.

In tracing genealogy in college they give you little figures like triangles and circles. It's very confusing for some of us — we know we can't portray our clan structure by means of triangles and circles. So I have borrowed a full chart from the Bureau of Indian Affairs to try to give you an idea of the relationship of clan and family members.

The center square in the chart represents either a boy or girl (Drawing 1). I'll put the mother to the right as you face the chart. The boy or girl automatically belongs to the

Father

Mother

Father's Clan

Mother's Clan

Boy   Girl

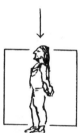

Male Members
Father Image

Male Members.
Brother Image

Teasing Cousins

Female Members
Aunt Image
(if same age),
Mother Image
(if older)

Female Members
Sister Image
(if same age),
Mother Image
(if older)

1. CROW Family and Clan Relationships

mother's clan. The male members of the mother's clan are in
the square underneath the mother. In the case of both boy
and girl, they take on a brother image regardless of their age;
in other words, they could be older or younger than the boy
or girl but they would still take on a brother image. The
relation of the female members of the mother's clan to the
boy and girl, on the other hand, depends on their age. If they
are in the same age group as the boy or girl, they take on the
sister image; if they are older, they take on a mother image.

I'll put the father to the left of the boy or girl, then the
male members of the father's clan who take on a father
image. Underneath the male members are the female members
of the same clan. They take on an aunt or mother image,
again depending on age.

Now the girl receives a certain amount of information
from the mother and the female members of the mother's
clan, such as how to make clothes and ornaments, how to
prepare food, take care of a home and all that. They
contribute to the more practical instruction of the girl. For
instance, as the girls are making moccasins, they teach them
that they should include good things in their thoughts, so that
wherever the moccasins tread, they will lead to good things in
life — good health and good days. The male members of the
mother's clan look on the girl as their sister, so not much
communication goes on between them. The things they speak
of among themselves would never be repeated in front of the
girl. The girl's actual brothers treat her the same way.

In the case of the boy, a certain amount of instruction
comes from the male members of the mother's clan, such as
how to go after game, how to handle horses, how to dress,
how to conduct yourself and what to seek in life. They also
teach the boy how to treat domestic animals. Even pets
understand kindness, and the clan brothers use that as an
example. For instance, if a dog is mistreated, it cringes every
time anyone speaks in a loud voice or indicates an act of
violence in its presence. But if the person is kind, he can go
through any motion or action, and the animal — despite the
fact that animals are considered to be dumb — recognizes that
he is to be trusted. Finally, the male members of the mother's

clan show the boy how to talk to women and what to look for in a woman. If they say, "You should go out and go after a woman," then you look for the qualities these people consider desirable. That's why wise men test those girls to see if they have the proper instructions and if they are good, reliable and respected.

We have different degrees of respect for different people. While a certain amount of advice comes from the parents and grandparents, it's mostly from the male and female members of the father's clan. They are the group that both the boy and girl learn to respect from childhood on. They give spiritual guidance and advice; at the same time, they're the ones who present the boy and girl to the public and try to build up their reputation. They're more or less their public relations people and the ones who make wishes and offer prayers for them. In other words, if a father wants prayers offered for his child, he'll go to these people. So they are the ones we respect and we try not to disappoint them by our conduct. They are also the ones we have to watch out for. We aren't supposed to pass in front of the members of our father's clan, for example, no matter how humble they may be.

The offspring of the male members of the father's clan are called 'Teasing Cousins.' They are the ones who remind the girl or boy who they are — who they actually are. The members of the father's clan, the public relations people, can go out in public and say, "We have the best boy among the whole tribe because he's smart, he behaves well, he listens." The teasing cousins say, "Baloney!" If they catch the boy telling a lie, they ridicule him in public. By being ridiculed in public, he refrains from telling lies. The same way with the girl. The girl may be brought out and told that she's a good respectable girl and shows good judgment. But some little incident is picked up by the teasing cousins and they say, "Baloney! She has no brains!" So morals are passed on to both girl and boy, and they learn to live by them.

When the child is born, the aunts on the father's side are responsible for providing the cradle, the little moccasins and any other clothing or part of the cradle that go to the child.

The wish that goes into the aunt's work as she makes those little moccasins is that the moccasins will be pointed toward good days, good luck, good health and well-being. If the child is in need of something, it's up to her to furnish it until that boy or girl reaches a certain age. It's also up to the aunt to provide something that's not common. For example, she usually preserves berries and things like that and probably uses them to make pudding or pemmican. Now it's up to her to give some of this to her niece or nephew. She puts in the best she has and offers it to the child. In so doing, the father of the child is obligated to give the aunt a gift, like a horse. The more he loves his child, the more valuable the gift. When he makes the gift, the aunt in turn makes a wish. She may have had a dream or vision of a certain season, so she makes a wish that the child will live to see that season.

The female members of the father's clan tell the girl what is desired in a woman and what she should remember — that she should not put this group to shame by her actions. They advise her on the value of chastity, the value of being a virtuous woman. But here comes the white man with a wonder drug — it's a foolproof contraceptive — so she forgets this information and tries to take a shortcut. This white man over here is telling the girl that by listening to her group, she's missing out on life. So by the introduction of the white man's contraceptives — and they're not foolproof — we have a lot of illegitimate children today, children without fathers. It's unbecoming for a young girl to have an illegitimate child. She puts a certain amount of shame on the female members of the father's clan, and she also does a disservice to her offspring. Although her child — let's say it's a boy — is still a member of the mother's clan, he doesn't have a father's clan. So he loses part of his identity. You might say he's almost like a man without a country. But if a girl wants to protect her child from this, if she wants to enjoy life and still keep in line with some of the things we hold dear in order to gain respect, the female members of the father's clan are the people she respects and follows.

ALLEN QUETONE: There were illegitimate children in our society even in the old traditional days, but they were few and far between because of the ties that made up the family unit, the band unit and the tribal unit. In the Kiowa tribe — and nobody taught me this, I just observed it — a mother who had given birth to an illegitimate child had the right to name the father. There was no question; he couldn't deny it. Even if he did deny it, the tribe accepted the mother's word so that the child had a father. The mother would say who the father was and the tribe would accept it, and from that day on that man's relatives took the youngster as their own and gave him the same honor, the same status as if he were the father's legitimate child.

But I believe the thing that helps most to maintain the Indian standards or behavior is our system of relationships. In the Kiowa tribe, Indian relations exist on a horizontal basis. There are three levels: father, grandfather, and brother and sister. All of our cousins are our brothers and sisters and therefore are due the same kind of treatment we accord our actual brothers and sisters. The same respect, the same honors, the same standards are applied to all of our cousins across the board. I think this is one of the mechanical things that influences the behavior of the Indian community.

It suddenly occurred to me while Henry was talking, that we were taught not to do or say certain things in front of our cousins or sisters. In other words, if they teach us not to do or say things to our sisters and they tell us that all these cousins are like our sisters, that same behavior applies to all of them. I think this is one way they had of controlling or at least of teaching us.

HENRY OLD COYOTE: You're going back to that thing my people stress — *respect.* They want you to respect others as you would like to be respected. It goes right back to that. The things that Stella and I discuss as a married couple, we would never discuss either with her brother or my sister or cousins.

ALLEN QUETONE: All risqué or off-color jokes are out in mixed company. Or I should say, not all mixed company, but your brothers and sisters and anyone else who belongs to a particular category. Where other relationships exist, certain things are allowed. For example, your brother's wives are your wives, not in the literal sense but in the sense that more is permitted between you in conversations and discussions.

HENRY OLD COYOTE: All of my wife's cousins or sisters claim me as their husband. When they get together, they don't say 'your husband,' they say 'our husband.' So I have more than one wife, but not in the literal sense of being a bigamist. By the same token, I don't have any boys of my own, so I claim all my brother's sons as my sons, though not in the sense in which the white man might interpret this. They all belong to me because they have my brother's blood in their veins. My brother and I have the same blood; we are of the same people, so my brother's offspring are part of me, also. They are my sons.

MAX HANLEY: The Navajos have the same type of relationships. All your brother's or sister's children call you 'little father.' They call you the same as your own sons. And it's just exactly like Henry said with the husbands.

We have teasing, too. After the baby starts walking and talking, that's where the big teasing comes in, except for your own sister. You have to be very respectful with her and talk to her in a certain way. Suppose you have a cousin; maybe it's your uncle's daughter. She can tease you and you can tease her. You can tease all the different relations you want, but you can't tease your sisters or brothers. You have to be very careful and very respectful about what you say to your sisters and brothers. They're the only ones you have to watch out for. You have to be very careful and know which people can't be teased.

When I go out in the field on the reservation, of course these people know me. I've come to visit them for a certain thing, not just for fun, so they know I'm coming for something very important. They all are quiet until someone speaks to me. Then they start teasing me like people do who are not related. Someone — maybe a lady, maybe a man, starts laughing. At first I don't say anything; I don't laugh. I've come there to see the ladies or men with something very important in mind. But when I start to smile a little bit, then they giggle.

I have three boys. When they were small we used to go

to different villages in Laguna or Zuni or Hopi country. I knew a lot of the people there. I knew them when they were young — now they are old, almost as old as I am. So my children watched how I talked to them and some of them would say, "Daddy, it looks as if you're pretty well known in almost every village." "Oh, yes. I got acquainted with all these people when I was in school." I spent 11 years down there in Sherman and Albuquerque and in Salt Lake and Intermountain and I used to go to summer school many times. That's where I got acquainted with these different tribes. Some of them came from South America and all the way from New York and some were Eskimos. So my children when they were small were surprised. "Did you go to all these places?" "No, I went to school with them down there. I spent 11 years in one place, then 2-3 years in another, then 5 years in another. That's the way I got acquainted with a lot of different tribes." For instance, when I go down to Laguna, they know me down there. Mrs. Loco, who lived at Laguna, was one of my old matrons at Sherman for many years. Vic says that she died recently. My wife and I visited her twice and she baked us corn bread years ago.

So different tribes recognize the kind of person you are. Some of these young Navajos call me 'brother' all the time, and I call them 'sisters.' If you call someone 'brother' or 'sister,' you have to treat him or her the same way you would your own brother and sister, even though you may not be related. This way more respect comes in. I know that I am meant to approach these people on the reservations I visit in a certain way; you've got to approach them according to where they stand. All of these things you have to learn among your own people.

ALLEN QUETONE: According to old Indian custom, when you take somebody for a brother or some other relation, what you're saying in effect is that you are going to treat that person the way you would if he were your blood brother or sister.

MAX HANLEY: One other thing I'd like to bring up is the special relation to your in-laws. My grandmother and my father don't see each other, because if you see your in-law, you're going to be blind before you get too old. Another lady says it's because it's shameful to look at your in-laws. There are these two reasons and I don't know which is true. I believe it's that you get blind, because when I got married, my wife's mother, who died about six years ago when she was 104 years old, said, "It's up to him. If he wants to be hiding from me, that's all right. I'll do likewise." But I said, "No, that's going to be a lot of trouble. I would rather see her and hear her story." So I went over there and saw her and we talked about this and that. Maybe that's why without glasses it's a little blurred. If I'd done otherwise, I might not have to wear eyeglasses. But somebody told me, "The reason you wear glasses is that pretty soon you will be 74 years old."

ARTHUR SUTTON: We've got one girl in our family now who's white — my daughter-in-law. We're teaching her that all our relations are her relations because she entered our home. Regardless of whether she's white or Indian, she gets the same respect, the same treatment. Now she's beginning to understand how we are related to different people and she takes them as her relations, too. So we are teaching her the Indian way. She says, "I want to learn because I'm one of you now. You're going to have to teach me." And I am going to teach her. She doesn't go to the women folks, so they talk about her. She comes to me and says, "Dad, you're going to have to teach me all these things." I told her, "I'll teach you certain things, but for the woman's part, you'll have to go to the older ladies." I just wanted to bring that out. Even though she's at a certain age, I'm going to have to give her the whole business from beginning to end, including the earlier teaching.

She's got a little boy now and she says, "I want this boy to have an Indian education to begin with, so he can know his Indian side. Later on he's going to have to learn my side." We're trying to teach that youngster so that he can know both sides, both cultures.

VICTOR SARRACINO: I'd like to explain the Laguna Pueblo version because that's the tribe from which I come. You will note that the tribes do have a variation of systems of behavior and so I'll add my portion to what's been said.

As you face my diagram, everything that relates to the woman goes on the left side and is marked by a circle because women believe in a circle most of the time. The men believe in squares, because in most of their prayers they refer to the four corners of the earth at all times. So, I will start by putting the grandmother on the upper left-hand corner and the grandfather on the upper right-hand corner (Drawing 2). The mother goes under the grandmother, and the father under the grandfather. From here on down there's a slight change. You have the sister of the mother and then the brother of the mother in the left-hand column, and the sister, then brother of the father, in the right-hand column. The girl is represented by the center circle and the boy by the square.

If you were to bring up a child, all these people would have to become child-centered; it's very important that everybody partake in the upbringing. As I mentioned earlier, soon after the boy begins to participate in any of the ceremonial activities, the second parents are established. This is where a change-over comes in. The man, a married man, becomes the father of the boy, and his wife becomes the mother as well. These are the ones who are responsible for providing the young boy with spiritual guidance. In turn, the brothers of both the mother and father have the job of teaching the boy a way of life, and respect and love. They usually don't have much to do with the young girl. Most of the advice that is given to the girl usually comes from three people — the mother, the sisters of the father and the sisters of the mother. If something unpleasant needs to be said, it comes from the sisters of both parents. These sisters are referred to as mothers of the girl. Now, when you get to the level of mother and father, the relation of mother and daughter is that of sisters. It's a sister relationship. The girl becomes a sister of the mother. This way they tend to get along much better. Otherwise the parent always has something over the girl by way of giving advice, giving orders, etc. This is why I said that children usually are not given commands. It's usually, "Could you please?" and "Would you?"

The overall responsibility for teaching the various members of the family to respect one another stems from the

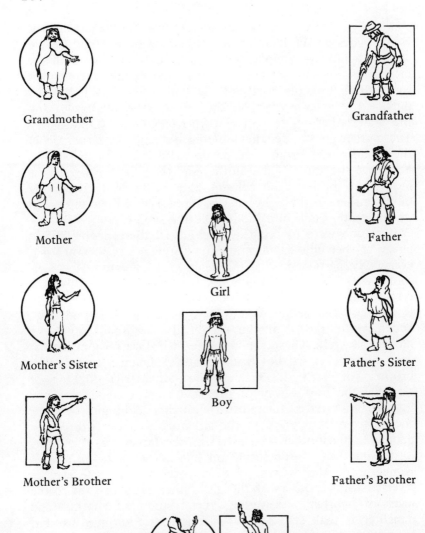

Grandmother

Grandfather

Mother

Father

Girl

Mother's Sister

Father's Sister

Boy

Mother's Brother

Father's Brother

Mother

Father

Second Parents

2. LAGUNA PUEBLO Family and Clan Relationship

grandmother and the grandfather. Our whole training in behavior starts from our grandparents (Drawing 3). To see that all is going well with the boy and girl, and also with the parents of the child, there are discussions first between the father and the grandfather, and between the mother and the grandmother. Then discussions take place between the grandmother and grandfather. They exchange the ideas and feelings of both parents. After these ideas have been exchanged, the messages are passed on to both father and mother. Let's say in this instance that the messages are passed on to the father. The mother relays the message to the grandmother, hoping that it will reach the father. That way many difficulties and misunderstandings are avoided. The two godparents also have direct contact with the grandparents — the grandparents are the ones they really communicate with. This is how information is relayed: to the grandparents, and through them to the father and mother. It is all this that keeps the family together.

Sometimes the parents have serious discussions at table when they're eating. Only in seriousness will the parents of the boy and girl discuss the question of respect and love while they're eating. They feel that all the good things the children are being taught will be digested as the good food is taken into the body.

I would also like to mention some of the beliefs we have with twins. I have a set of twins, and a lot of people say that you have to treat these twins as extra-special; they also feel that a lot of luck will come to these two. We always automatically call twins, 'The Great Warrior' and 'The Man of Wisdom and Intelligence.' The first born is usually the Great Warrior and the Brave One, and the second born is Intelligence and the Person of Wisdom. So these are the names my twins have.

JOHN GARDNER: This reminds me of the Greeks. As you may know, there are two twins in Greek mythology who are called Prometheus and Epimetheus. Prometheus was the valiant and warrior-like one who stole the fire from the gods, and Epimetheus was the one who was thoughtful and reflective and full of wisdom.

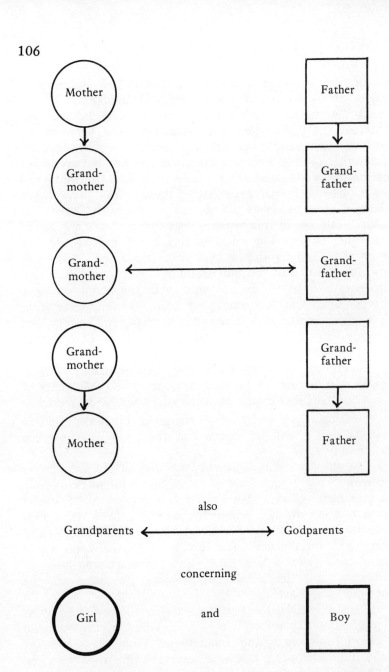

LAGUNA PUEBLO. Family Communication Flow

VICTOR SARRACINO: We have many traditions about the Great Warrior and the Man of Wisdom and Intelligence. These two persons were known to travel all around the world, thus they are connected with the East Coast, the Pacific Coast and the Artics. There's even a legend that if they wanted to disturb the lightning and thunder, they could do so.

As far as my own twins are concerned, I really haven't treated them as extra-special; I treat them the way I treat my other children. These two were born on May 13 on a Friday, and they have pulled many good twists on me. Let me give you two examples. The boys are both in the same class at school, and the teachers have already tried to split them up, but they haven't succeeded. One day the school team was going to Albuquerque to run in a race. One of them was selected to go and the other wasn't, so he felt kind of bad. He looked at me and said, "Daddy, I can't go to the race; just Melvin was picked," and he gave me that kind of look that said, "I'll fix them." They went into the next room and I guess they came up with some plan. Anyway, the one twin said, "You know, Melvin is going to get sick tomorrow, so I've got to substitute for him. You'd better tell that teacher." Sure enough, the next day Melvin was coughing and all that. So my wife went up there and told the teacher that the one who had been picked couldn't go but that his brother was going to substitute for him. There was a big fuss. They had to see the principal and the teacher, but finally they agreed to take him. Then about one hour after the team had left, the other boy said, "Mom, I'm not sick. We were just doing that. You've got to take me. I've got to run in that race." And she had to take him, too!

A week later the other boy got sick. He was coughing, so we told him not to go to school. His twin went, and after he got home he said, "Mom, I did my school work and I did homework in school for my brother, so he and I don't have to go to school tomorrow. We've got all that taken care of." They do little things like that each day. They're really something to watch when they're playing. They come up with a problem and they solve it immediately, because there are two of them all the time; they reason these things out together.

MAX HANLEY: We have a special belief as to how children become twins. In the past, the Navajos had to move around a great deal. The father and mother stayed in one place that they called summer camp. Then in winter they had to go higher up to camp, maybe on the mesa, where there are more trees and more grass. When it came time to move to winter camp, they'd get the grinding stone to store it away. Now, maybe there are two or three hogans in that summer camp, and each one has a grinding stone. Let's say you've got two grinding stones: one belongs to one lady, the other to another lady. If you put these two together and store them away somewhere, sure enough you're going to get a pair of twins later on. That's why my people are really superstitious about this. They always try to set those grinding stones apart when they store them — one maybe in front, the other someplace else.

Now, I have two brothers, John and Thomas, who are twins. I was already grown-up when they were born. They're 59 now, and this coming September I'll be 74. Mother called the first boy, 'Gray Boy,' the second boy's name is 'Red Boy.'' When they started walking and running around, they both actually looked alike. If my mother wanted these boys to do certain things, she couldn't tell which was which. So she wouldn't look at the boys. She'd pretend she was doing something. "Red Boy;" she'd say, "Go over there and do this." One would look at the other and say, "It's you!" Then she'd look at them. "Which one's Red Boy?" "Him!" "Him!" So she made both of them go; both at the same time.

My mother and father trained these two little kids, John and Thomas, and showed them how to handle horses, and how to look after cows and sheep and donkeys. These four things were the most important part of training them. Then the boys grew up. They got married and they're doing fine. They've been taught pretty well, and they always mention — especially Thomas — how they were trained through their grandmother and uncles. Here's one of them working on a farm. He takes charge of the young Navajos out in the field where they use tractors, cultivate the fields, bale hay and so forth. The other one, Thomas, is teaching these little ones in day school. Also, he knows something about the Navajo culture through the grandfather they used to call Braidy. His name was Braidy because he used to have braidy hair. So I always remember how these two boys were raised. They have no gray hair, almost like me, and they're still able to do lots of things.

ERNEST BENEDICT: Our people are divided into clans. These clans are really rather extended families, where the relationship is determined through the women of the communities and not through the men. There's very little relationship through the men. For instance, my father and his brothers and sisters are relatives, but they each have their own names. My real family, my closest relatives, are on my mother's side. Quite often in my travels, either on the home reservation or some neighboring reservations, I get inquiries as to the health of my mother and some of my relatives on my mother's side, and then secondly, perhaps, of my father.

I belong to the Wolf Clan. Somehow or other the Wolf Clan seems to have survived better than the other Mohawk clans, so we have quite a large membership compared with the two other main clans, the Bear and the Turtle. There are three minor clans, which seem to have a large membership, but they don't have the political or social status. These are the Little Turtle, the Snipe and the Eel or Ball Clan — there's some difference of opinion as to how to translate the names of the latter two clans. They are ceremonial names, which makes it hard to identify the actual objects or symbolism the names represent.

HENRY OLD COYOTE: Could it be that the names of these clans have been lost through the fact that the meaning of the word has changed or is no longer understood? Among our own people there are some expressions that don't have much meaning any more to the younger set. For instance, the name of the charm they use for an otter is different from the present-day reference to an otter. The present word for otter doesn't sound anything like the word they used to use. First it sounded like the word for a book being turned over; later on they used a term for otter that is similar to the word for 'bug.' So when you start using the old terms, the younger set are a little confused. Maybe that's what has happened to the names of your clans — maybe the meaning has been lost along the way.

ERNEST BENEDICT: That's possible, because some of the old people say that the names have changed meaning and that the younger child cannot remember these old words.

In spite of these and other changes, we try to keep alive a certain number of traditions. The family is still extended to include all the members of a clan. Nowadays the Mohawk men are mostly construction workers. They work in cities and commute on weekends to see their families, so the mother of the family is still the person who holds the family together and regulates the relations between that family and other families. The Iroquois women play an important role in today's society. They actually hold the community together while the men are away working. So there's a real use for this old traditional form of clan mothers and clan memberships. Quite often the women are the most vocal people in local politics, though most of the actual chiefs are men. Very few women hold office, even in modern-day elected councils. Still, they let the women do a lot of the talking in the councils.

We also have the tradition of the uncles taking over much of the training of the young boys — that is, the brothers of the mother. Of course, in the absence of uncles, the father sets the example for the young lad. The boy is taught mainly by example, by being able to follow along with the grownups. Very little training is done by older boys, but, I think the older girls almost naturally become the teachers of their younger sisters. They carry them around, take care of them, check their diapers and everything. The older boys, on the other hand, are not the teachers of the younger boys, but the uncles are. And sometimes the uncles are not much older than the boys themselves.

The only thing I would like to add is that when a man married, he was never permitted to confront his mother-in-law. If they came together, she covered her face. Still the mother-in-law was expected to remain with the children as a part of the family. The son-in-law had his own work to do and was probably absent from the village anyway, so they seldom ran into each other.

ARTHUR SUTTON: In our way, we're not supposed to talk to our mother-in-law or with our sisters. We're silent, but we still treat them with great respect. We don't want to mistreat them, or have anyone else mistreat them.

VICTOR SARRACINO: What we do at home seems to resolve a lot of problems. The wife usually goes to her in-law's home, where the newly married couple are encouraged to live rather than immediately to build a new home. They tend to live with the boy's family, then little by little, they start building their home.

HENRY OLD COYOTE: Some historians and writers refer to the custom of not speaking to your mother-in-law as a taboo of some sort: that if you talk to your mother-in-law something will happen, like you won't get game. But that's not the case, and Mr. Sutton just covered it. It's a sign of respect. And it doesn't stop with the mother-in-law. According to our custom, I can't speak to my wife's brother's wife. That's also a custom of respect. In return, she can't talk to my brother-in-law, my sister's husband, unless it's necessary. In other words, there may be times when my brother-in-law comes around; he may be hungry, but if she's alone, there's no way of communicating. In order to avoid that kind of situation, I made her give my brother-in-law a horse. So they shook hands and, instead of addressing her as a sister-in-law, he now addresses her as sister. I did the same thing with both my sisters-in-law. I gave them presents and shook hands with them and I now address them as sisters. It's a sign of respect. Even though you don't talk to them before exchanging gifts, you still respect them. And when you take care of the obligation to the extent of giving them gifts, you still respect them. So this popular belief that if you talk to your mother-in-law you're going to itch, or you're not going to be able to get game, couldn't be further from the truth.

There are also cases where an emergency arises. Once my sister got sick, and there were just two others with her — my mother and my sister's husband. In that emergency, my mother addressed my brother-in-law. They broke that barrier,

but they took care of the obligation afterwards. After the
emergency was over, she gave my brother-in-law some gifts,
including a horse. So even though they broke the tradition,
they still took care of it at a later date.

The same thing is done if a mistake is made. A blunder
of my brother-in-law cost me a horse. What he was trying to
do was to name that pemmican that he had in his hand, but
he stumbled and said my mother's Indian name instead.
Everybody laughed and he was embarrassed. The next day I
went and got the horse, and my mother gave it to him, so
he's free to call her name now.

ERNEST BENEDICT: One of the ways of showing
respect among our people is to speak to all people who are
older than you by approximately a generation as uncles and
aunts, whether they are actually related or not. Then, if there
are some who are even older than that, they are called
grandparents, whether they are in the same clan or not. On
my own age level, I am obligated to speak to people of my
own clan as brothers and sisters and to those of my age from
other clans, as cousins. In a formal gathering like a council
meeting, however, everybody at the same age level is brother
and sister. I call those who are younger than I nephews and
nieces, if they are members of my clan; again, depending on
the closeness of the relationship, I might even call them my
own children. They are obligated to address people on my age
level as uncles and aunts and there is one special expression
for that in the Mohawk language. The current generation are
being taught that expression, and in some cases — very few
cases — they're using it. It's a very polite expression, which
has become quite rare, because of the fact that most of my
own generation speak only English. But there's a new interest
in the Mohawk language and it makes me very happy when I
hear young people of this newer generation using the old
forms, some of which are unfamiliar to me. These are polite
and very good words. You might call them classical
expressions that are remembered and are used in the Council.
They are used very carefully and very reverently.

11

THE HOME

HENRY OLD COYOTE: The dwelling of the Plains Indian is the tipi. It is made from wooden poles and buffalo hide and is shaped like a cone with two outside flaps, which we call smoke flaps or ventilators, that protrude from the top above the entrance. The door of the tipi faces east, and on the outside, opposite the door, are two poles controlling the ventilators (Drawing 1). The Crow tipi is built around four basic poles* that are set around a wide circle on the ground.** These four poles represent the four points of the compass: east, south, west and north. In addition to these four, there are subordinate poles, the number of which depends on the size of the tipi.*** The bigger the tipi, the more poles you use. Seventeen or eighteen, including all the poles (the base poles, the ventilator poles, etc.) is about the

---

*Indians of different tribes were known as either "three-pole people" or "four-pole people," according to the number of poles which formed the basic foundation on which the other poles rested. The Blackfeet, the Crows, the Hidatsas, or Gros Ventres of the Village, the Commanches, Omahas, the Sarsis, close to Blackfeet, the Flatheads, Kutenais, and Nez Perces were all four-pole people. Tribes using the three-pole tipi included the Sioux, Cheyennes, Arapahos, Assiniboines, Kiowa, Gros Ventres of the Prairie, Plains-Cree, Mandans, Arikaras, Pawnees and Omahas. *Ed.*

**The four-pole foundation gives the tipi more of an oval shape than the three-pole tripod. The four poles form the corners of a rectangle, the narrow sides of the rectangle facing east and west, as a rule. *Ed.*

***The inside diameter of the tipi ranges from approximately 10 to 30 feet. *Ed.*

114

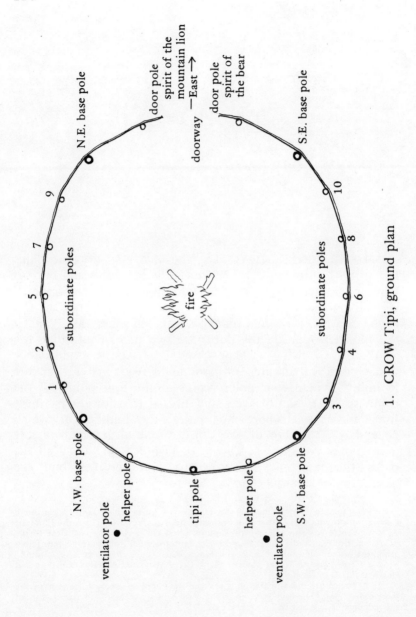

1. CROW Tipi, ground plan

minimum number, and twenty-three is about the maximum. The four base poles are the only poles that are tied. They are tied together with a stout rawhide thong, and the remaining poles are placed upon these four with their top portion interwoven in a criss-cross pattern which goes from the back to the doorway of the tipi. What we call the fork of the tipi is the point of intersection of the poles.

We number the subordinate poles in the following way, because they represent things of varying degrees of importance. The number one pole is to the left of the northwest base pole and the number two pole is next to number one. Then we jump across to the other side of the tipi where the number three pole is to the right of the southwest base pole and the number four pole is next to number three. Number five pole is next to number two, number six next to number four, seven next to five and so on, criss-crossing back and forth across the circumference of the tipi. At the back opposite the door, we have what we call the tipi pole, which is the chief or center pole, and two helper poles on either side of it. The number of these three remains constant; whatever the size of the tipi, there are never fewer or more. On each side of the door you have a door pole and, of course, you have the two outside poles controlling the smoke flaps. The fire is usually located in the center of the tipi for practical reasons. From this location, the smoke can easily go out of the smoke hole at the top; also, since the tipi is flammable, a fire in the center of the tipi is well out of reach of the poles and cover.

According to legend, there was a man who brought back the design for the tipi after he had encountered and slain certain undesirable characters. He saw that Old Man, the Sun, and was told that he had been selected because he was a good man and a good warrior. His name was Yellow Leggings. Yellow Leggings had a pet, a bear. When he came back from that Old Man, he informed the people that the spirit of the bear should remain and guard one side of the door and so he tied the bear to one of the door poles. He also told them that on his way back he had run across seven brothers who had decided to turn themselves into something that was

Smoke flaps
A. Spirit of the Owl
B. Spirit of the Coyote

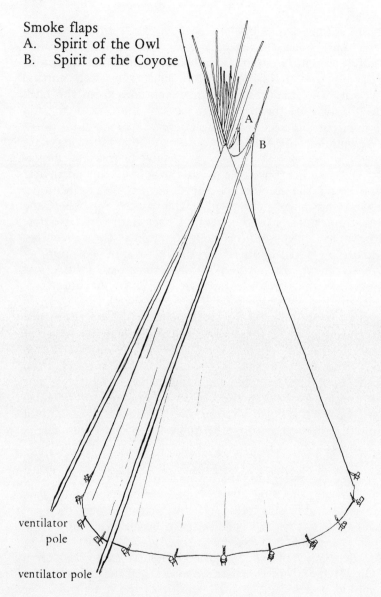

2. CROW Tipi seen from S.S.W.

permanent. In deciding, they said that even things like rocks crumble, but if they were to reside in the sky as the seven stars in the Big Dipper, they would remain forever. So they left this world to reside in the Big Dipper. Now the youngest brother told his brother-in-law, Yellow Leggings, that he would leave behind on earth the spirit of his pet, the mountain lion, to guard the other side of the tipi, and so he tied it to the other door pole. Both the bear and the mountain lion guard the tipi at night. Facing east, the lion is on your left and the bear on your right. The bear is regarded as a fearsome animal; the evil forces stay away because of their fear of it. The mountain lion is also regarded as a fearsome beast.

Each part of the tipi has a meaning. As you face east, the left smoke flap represents the spirit of the owl who watches over the tipi at night; the right flap represents the spirit of the coyote who watches over the tipi by day (Drawing 2). The owl and coyote are sentries; the bear and mountain lion are protectors. In addition, the base pole that faces northeast represents the spirit that controls the day coming over from the east; the one that faces southeast, the eternal summer; the one facing southwest, the point where people leave the world and follow the Old Man over the horizon; and the one to the northwest represents the eternal winter, where the weather comes and freshens the earth. They also represent the four seasons of the year.

The tipi pole represents the owner of the tipi, and the other poles represent important things in the owner of the tipi's life. What elements or forces the owner selects are personal, but they are always connected with nature. The number one thing that is important, for example, could be the environment, the next could be the storms, the next, the rains or waters of the earth, then the different animals or birds, and so forth. If we use our drawing as a model, he can choose up to ten things that are important and address himself to them as he faces each pole. Because the poles are made of wood, they also represent the trees. What the Indian is doing is surrounding himself with the symbols of the environment. The idea is this: Just as the tipi poles come together, so do the forces they represent converge and shelter the Indian who stands beneath them. The Indian lives under this great power.

The practice of paying homage to the various elements, which the tipi represents, varies from individual to individual. Usually, the man of the house addresses those elements in the order of importance which he attaches to each thing, or in the sequence in which they properly come. For instance, he may turn to the four base poles to address the seasons according to the proper sequence in which they unfold. He makes a wish for a good life in each season, because he wants to be able to walk in those seasons. He finishes by paying his respects to Mother Earth on which he stands, and which forms the floor of his home. In the course of his homage, the Indian uses the pipe, so that the smoke he exhales, which acts as a medium, will carry his prayers upward.

The area between the northwest and southwest poles is known as the 'place of respect.' It is where the Indian keeps his personal medicine bundle (Drawing 3). Because the things which the medicine bundle represents may be violated in the tipi during the day, the keeper of the bundle takes it outside in the morning. He walks clockwise — which is the direction in which the sun journeys through the sky — from the northwest to the northeast pole out the door, and continues in this clockwise direction. When he wants to bring the medicine bundle in at night, he walks again in a clockwise direction, enters the doorway, and moves from the southeast to the southwest pole where he puts the bundle back on the center pole in the place of respect.

The tipi always faces east. When the Indian goes out in the morning to face the Old Man, he takes four steps outside the tipi as he faces the new day. The sun is the Old Man coming up over the east. He faces that Old Man, then he turns to his right. By turning to the right, he anticipates the path of the sun; he has gotten ahead of it and taken care of facing it even before it has reached the western horizon. He does this once in the day, the first time he comes out. The rest of the time, he can run in and out of the tipi as he pleases. Chances are he's a very forgetful man and has left all his tools in there! But the following day he faces a new day again. He takes those four

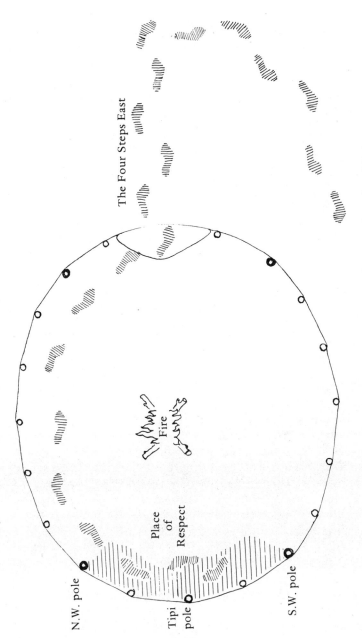

3. CROW Ritual Movement Pattern Leaving Tipi

steps, makes a wish for each step and each season of the year
that lies ahead, makes that turn to the right, then goes about his
business. This way, he feels that he can't go back to yesterday,
he can't go back to last season; he looks forward. He wants a
good day, just like today is a good day. In Indian life there is no
such thing as a bad day. Even if it's stormy, every day is good.
If you are alive, it is a good day!

In the old days they used to weight down the tipi with
rocks. When the Indian moved, he took only his tipi with him
and left these rocks. That's why you find a lot of tipi rings out
in the Plains. Once there was an Indian boy who was thrown off
this cliff; he hung on to a little juniper tree until some Big Horn
sheep came along and rescued him. The sheep brought him back
to safety and more or less adopted him; they gave him certain
powers, and the various animals in the area began contributing
to this boy. They told him he would outlive four generations,
and he did. We even have his burial site. It's not exactly a shrine
in the white man's sense, but I can remember as a boy leaving
little beads at that grave. Anyway, he learned something that
was to affect the way the tipi was set up. The Badger told him
that any time he sank his claws into the ground, nothing could
budge him. So the boy came up with the idea of tent pegs.
From that boy's time on, the Indians switched from using rocks
to tent pegs, because the boy had learned from the badger that
if you stick something fast in the ground, you can't move it.

These pegs are often used to identify the family living in a
particular tipi. For example, one family might peel the bark of a
peg back to a particular point, or carve one or several rings
around it; they might paint it with a stripe of a particular color,
or use a particular type of wood. Some might use red willow,
some ash, some chokeberry. My own family is supposed to use
red willow. Some of these families that mark their tent pegs also
mark the four base poles with their own colors. My family and
my wife's family take the elk as our patron; it's from this
animal that we get our help. In addition, my grandfather gave us
the weasel. Then we have the eagle, and both my wife and I
have the Sacred Tobacco. We keep and use the colors that go
with these animals or objects; we use red paint, and blue, and
yellow, and sometimes green. We don't take any old paint the

way they do in Hollywood when they make movies about Indians. For instance, when you put red paint on your face, it represents the red sunrise and the red sunset. You are imitating the Old Man by putting red paint on your face. You are saying it's going to be a good day following the red sunset, and you are asking for a good day. When I go into a ceremony, I put yellow on my face and arm, and blue lightning on my body, according to what was revealed in a vision. Each of these colors represents something of significance, whether I use them on my body or in my home.

When Indians marry and move into their first home, they are not the first to enter it. They get their clan uncles to go in ahead of them and make wishes for them. A crier goes in together with the clan uncles and announces to those elements and forces that are represented in the tipi that this newly-married couple is about to move in; these young people are going to make this their first home and it is going to be a home of plenty and of long life. After these little wishes have been made, the young couple extend an invitation to someone to visit them; they have to make this invitation first, and only afterwards do they have the right to move in. Nowadays this tradition is being used for houses, too, since Indians no longer live in tipis all year round.

The tipi itself represents a woman. The belief is that you can lose your mother — your mother is on loan to you from the Great Father — but as long as you have a place to come home to where you can find security and happiness, you have a second mother. After I found out the significance of the tipi, I learned to respect it. I knew that it represents the woman and that every day as you face a new day, you are born all over again. You learn to respect the fact that a human being has no roots, that his soul just barely touches the surface of the earth. You know, too, that your body is part of the earth, that this part of you comes from the earth and is going to return to it. So every day you make peace with the earth. Thus, when you address Mother Earth, you are actually addressing yourself.

It is a woman's role to make and take care of the tipi. She decides what the size of the tipi will be. The man goes out and gets the hides, and she tans them with the help of her relatives.

She decides about the structure, how many paces there should be between the poles and how to arrange the hides. The average tipi would take about 18 buffalo hides, which would make it approximately 20 feet in diameter and 20 feet high.

The women are trained for this role already at a very early age. When they are little girls, they play house — they have their own little tipi and they make miniature camps. Then when the women make a new tipi, they usually ask the young girls to go and get different sweet smelling plants, like sweet sage, to make a smudge inside the tipi. It's the young girls' chore, and it purifies and sweetens the air. From the time they are able to walk around, they are exposed to this procedure of setting up and preparing the tipi. When the older women set up the tipi, the little girls help to drive down the stakes, to move the poles around, to put the lining on the inside. The women stress neatness, and it's usually the most skilled women who put the lining up, so that it's even all the way around.

ALLEN QUETONE: I might add a word here concerning the pride of workmanship that goes into anything an Indian makes. The Kiowas, and I think most tribes are the same in this respect, take great pride in doing things right. If your work is good, it will be held up as a standard of high quality. Conversely, poor workmanship will probably bring some amount of ridicule. If you have things that are not of quality workmanship, chances are people will go around making faces and whispering remarks. This negative response tends to have the effect of bringing out the best people have to offer in the total scheme of things. Even at this stage of the breakdown of our culture, when we use other standards and wear white men's clothes, there is still a certain amount of pride in quality. Even though we drive the same car as the white man, and wear his clothes, and speak his language, we still maintain our own standards. In one sense, this is what puts our kids so far behind in school. They are still guided by Indian standards and attitudes, which are different from the white man's. Vic was saying last night that a comparison was made between the performance of Indian school kids from two different pueblos, one of which was more traditional than the other. The kids from the traditional pueblo were not showing up well in the tests, and the teacher was saying that these kids were dumb. But as Vic remarked, give those kids a test in Indian, and they'll make straight A's. That brings me to the subject of Pueblo workmanship and how you build your homes. Vic, would you describe this for us?

VICTOR SARRACINO: To begin with, the Laguna tribe has always understood this earth to be its mother, so we relate everything back to Mother Earth when we build our homes. When an individual wishes to build, a request is first made to that person known as White Hands. White Hands is in charge of giving out assignments for building homes. He is a religious type of person who prays all day long, and prior to making this assignment he goes into meditation. Once he has made the assignment, he is shown where the site is. The gentleman immediately goes into a prayer and asks the Supreme God for forgiveness that these people are going to dig into the ground. Then when the boundary is established, White Hands goes out and blesses it with either corn pollen or corn meal or charm stones. He blesses one corner and makes a mark similar to the sign of the cross, representing the four corners of the earth. Then he blesses another corner and makes another mark. He goes counterclockwise from the north until he has blessed each corner; then he makes an entry from the eastern corner to the middle and he makes a blessing in the center. While he stands there, he sends a blessing into the underworld and to the upper world, then he turns back to the center where he makes a final blessing and gives the word to proceed.

There is a long story behind White Hands. He is the person who led his people to the promised land where the Pueblos live. Until recently, there has always been a successor, an individual who was given this name. About a hundred years ago, White Hands went out of existence as a leader, but there were others who were appointed to carry out his tasks. The only ones used now are war captains or chiefs, though they mention the name of White Hands. But even the name is becoming extinct.

After White Hands has blessed the site where the individual plans to build, the whole family gets together and all agree that they will pitch in and help the ones whose home it is to be. In the meantime, they begin the digging of the foundation in a

124

4. LAGUNA PUEBLO. Blessing of Laguna Pueblo Home. Arrowhead is
placed to point west in each corner of foundation

counterclockwise direction; as soon as it is done, the individuals to whom the pueblo will belong go to the village officers. The latter are the people in charge of the distribution of water for irrigation and of native materials, such as rock, timber, and soil or dirt mortar. Unless they give you permission to use this material, that site may be sitting there for a long time, but usually they agree to give you everything at a low cost.

When approximately two feet of the foundation has been built and the permit for these native materials is given, the young man's family goes out and gathers the rocks and brings them in and piles them up. Then, of course, the women folk on the wife's side agree that the ladies will do the plastering. So the work is shared between the men and the women. As soon as the foundation is built, one of the religious leaders is called in to bless it. He brings four arrowheads along with him and starts by giving a blessing toward the north as before, but this time he lays an arrowhead in the northeast corner. He proceeds in a counterclockwise direction, placing an arrowhead in each corner and blessing it. Each arrowhead faces west (Drawing 4). Then he goes to the center of the site, says his prayers, gives the house a blessing and steps out. Once the ceremony is over, the people can continue to build again.

These pueblos usually have all their doorways facing east so that the inhabitants can meet the rising sun each day and ask for blessings for the new day. As Henry said, every day is a good day, and all you need to do is adjust yourself to the weather. If it's windy, you adjust yourself to the wind; if it's rainy, to the rain; but whatever is happening to that day, it is always a good day. As they build, they always put two windows on the east side (Drawing 5). In the old days before we used glass, my people used glass-like rocks or crystals instead. Next the beams are laid. Usually there are anywhere from 12 to 24, and they are made of baby pine. Then smaller timbers are laid at an angle on either side of the beams in an arrow or herring-bone design. Finally, they lay little twigs on top and cover them with regular dirt mortar or adobe mud. So the pueblo is covered with adobe, which keeps it cool during the hot summer months and warm during the wintertime.

Like the Plains Indians, my people treat the home as a

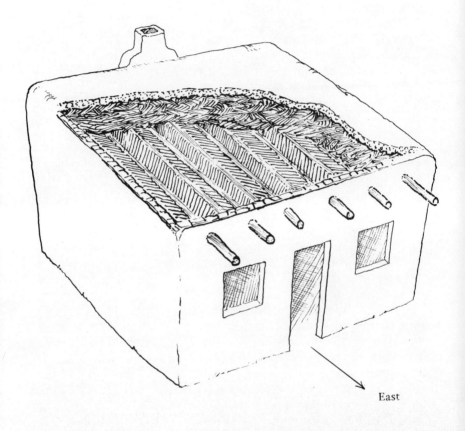

East

5. LAGUNA PUEBLO. Adobe Home showing roof
construction

woman, in our case because it is made from Mother Earth. These buildings are sacred, and we treat them as such. The four walls represent the four seasons as well as the four corners of the earth. On the reservation at Laguna, we also use colors for each of the directions. East is white, north is yellow, orange or red; west is blue, and south is green. At the top or roof, it's crystal — crystal clear; at the bottom it's black; and right in the middle it's all colors combined into one. Although we don't actually color the building, we know that each direction contains its own color. While we pray, we keep in mind the fact that the directions have these colors in them; that is why our prayers have so much beauty.

This is as much as I am allowed to tell you about how the house is structured and built. Every home in Laguna has a fireplace; the fireplace is significant to my people, but it is something I cannot discuss, because it has to do with different religious societies. I have never been initiated into the Charcoal group or anything that has to do with fire. Also, there is more to building the kiva* than to the home itself, because a lot of the religious activities and dancing take place in it. But again I am not permitted to discuss the kiva. Even if I were, it is still difficult to convey a complete picture of the Pueblo attitude toward the home and building. I think the Indian view is always of the total thing, not of just a fragment here and there, and I believe a great deal of misunderstanding is caused by the fact that we look at things differently than white people.

JOHN GARDNER: Just a remark about that total view. In so short a conference, we can hardly treat even one subject in depth. We can hardly go into the real significance of the building of a home, because there are many aspects of it, and some of them you are not free to discuss. Thus your remarks about the tipi and the home have to stand in our conference simply as symbols of how an Indian child is brought to value the meaning of life. White people think a lot about 'the meaning of life' in a general, abstract way. But we actually do many things mechanically, without much feeling for the significance of each detail. Only after the practical things are done mechanically, do we sit and ponder about the meaning of

---

*The kiva is a separate structure and a sacred place of worship. *Ed.*

life in general. But this is abstract, and not very fruitful. You have shown that the Indians, on the other hand, find real meaning in each different part of the tipi or pueblo or hogan, and in every step of building it. It is for this reason that they find meaning in the sum of all the things they do; that is, in life as a whole. They won't need at the end of the day to sit down and wonder if life has a meaning, because they have had nothing but meaning all the day through.

But think of the kind of education children are getting today. What in our schools would they be taught about building a house? They would be taught that the foundation has to be strong enough to hold up the walls — this would be a technical and mathematical problem that would have to be worked out. Then they would be told that you have to have the right materials and the proper adhesives — this would be a problem of physics and chemistry. They would be taught that the purpose of shelter is to keep out rain and snow, that you should build a house so that it's comfortable, and that you should figure out the cheapest and fastest and easiest way of doing it. That's about as far as the meaning goes. And since the house really doesn't have any meaning in itself, it may just as well be done as cheaply and fast and easily as possible, because thus we can save our attention for the meaning of life somewhere else — a somewhere that never appears!

What interests us is to figure out how we can follow the Indian example so that not only in house-building, but in other areas too, children can become awake to the inner meaning behind outer events in every aspect of their studies. To teach young children as you do affects their character, their disposition, their outlook, their intentions. You train them not only to be technically competent; you give them moral and spiritual training at the same time and on the same project. In our present civilization, however, everything is technical and economic. Technique, mechanics and money lack the magic and mystery that obviously infuse every detail of traditional Indian life.

ALLEN QUETONE: Probably the first thing the Indian child is made aware of is the mystery of existence. He learns this first and learns how to build a house second. His whole learning process is begun only after becoming aware of the mystery of all that is around him, strictly from a feeling point of view. He is encouraged to do this, and later, when he learns about specific things, he recognizes the spirit force within them.

HENRY OLD COYOTE: Some of the young Indians today who have been sent to white schools and deprived of this teaching, are showing some interest in it, especially in the Indian Studies Program. Some children never had the chance to learn these things, but they are getting it now. As I've said before, with television and record players and what have you, children don't have the time to receive this period of instruction at home, and the parents are usually too busy. They depend on the teachers, but the teachers don't know these things. But now that the Indian Studies Program is being introduced into the classroom, Indian children are again being exposed to this way of thinking, and they are showing interest. They feel better and more confident by knowing something about their background, and they are beginning to speak up and get good grades.

JIMMY BEGAY: Most of the Navajo schools have similar programs and are awakening to the need to give youngsters more of this kind of training in Navajo culture, language and so forth. It is being done not only to better the children in school, but also to give them a better understanding of their heritage and of their relationship to the dominant society.

ERNEST BENEDICT: Among the Mohawks, a feeling for things such as the sacredness of the home is pretty well gone, and pretty well frustrated by all that has happened to us and been taught to us. Nowadays the child is usually born in a hospital outside the reservation, although government officials stress the importance of the Indian's ties to his reservation. The child is sent away to school, where he is taught how important the home is and how essential it is for the family to stay together all the time! So here you have the Indian child in an outside environment, trying to cope among strangers, and at the same time being instructed to be proud of his home, his family, his reservation. It doesn't make much sense to us, and we find it pretty hard to figure what this white society is all about.

SYLVESTER MOREY: What most of you have said about the home and its sacredness tells not only white educators but parents as well that homes would be more peaceful and problems with children less, if the children were given the feeling that there is something truly sacred about the home in which they live. There is a real lesson here for us to take to white people.

JOHN GARDNER: You have shown us what the old way had to offer. The old way was based in religion 24 hours a day. Religion touched all things; it was a way of life, not a set of creeds or doctrines or principles practiced only on Sunday. But this religious attitude has been a way of life for all peoples, not just for Indians. Within America, however, we are cut off from the European backgrounds, and Asiatic and African backgrounds, where religion was such a dominant force in the past. Within America, it is above all the American Indians who stand for the old way, the spiritual way, and it is therefore they who can bring wisdom to the non-Indians in this country at this time.

All the same, you can't go backwards. Even if all non-Indians had the utmost reverence for what the Indians have done, they couldn't say, "Okay, let's all be Indians. Let's all build tipis. Let's all go back to the forests or to the plains." We can't do that. So in the end what both of us are facing is a question about the future — the Indians, because they have a very hard lot in life and uncertain prospects; the non-Indians, because they too have a hard lot, which they have brought upon themselves. Their prospects are getting more uncertain every day. I believe that in everything you say, you show us how the spiritual element can be woven into life, and that without it life has no meaning. It remains for us to find the kind of education for the future that will bring the spirit back into all the practical aspects of American civilization.

12
NATURE

VICTOR SARRACINO: In the area in which I live, people have great respect for all living creatures on this earth. While many of our neighboring tribes rely on the buffalo for food and clothing, the Pueblos rely on the deer for the food that it brings and the clothing it provides. There are many religious ceremonies performed not only for luck in the hunt, but in tribute to the deer on whom we depend for the necessities of life. One week before a big hunt, there are various groups that have their own dances and ceremonies in which all those who are going on the hunt participate, because dancing is one of the ways of expressing good wishes. At these dances, special songs are sung from early in the evening until midnight. Our people use corn meal, corn pollen and charm stones to bless these preparations, and it is the women who make sure that enough fresh corn pollen and meal are available. They do the grinding and they also cut the charm stones, such as turquoise, into small pieces. Everything has to be freshly made, freshly done; it can't have been sitting around for a year or two. During the purification period prior to the hunt, all the men fill their hearts with respect for the community and their leaders, and for the women folk. Before setting out, they are supposed to have only one thought in mind, and this is the good things out in the mountain; with this good thought they are led out into the mountain.

Upon reaching the hunting ground, each man cleans the area where he will sleep, as well as the fireplace and the place where he will hang his luck. Each one offers prayers, and again corn pollen is used. Then the men get together and sing a song, after which each of them goes off in one of four directions and tries to find the highest hill or peak in the area toward which he is headed. Upon reaching that peak, each man finds an evergreen tree and cleans underneath it and takes this fluffy little eagle feather that he carries with him. He places it right at the top of the evergreen tree, as it was done when he was a young boy. This fluffy feather serves as the messenger to the Almighty Supreme God, who is the provider of all things, and conveys the fact that the hunter is there for one purpose — to receive blessing in getting food plus all the things that go along with it. After he has addressed the Almighty, he goes off to hunt, and in many instances it doesn't take long to make a kill.

If an individual kills a deer, he gives a howl so that everybody in the area will hear it. After the kill, he lays the deer in an easterly direction, or, as we always say, in the direction of the rising sun. All those people in the distance who hear this yell, go to where he is and offer prayers and praise the man who made the kill. Of course, everyone is happy, and whoever gets near the deer gives it a blessing.

The person who is to skin the deer makes an imaginary mark indicating where he is going to cut, starting with the four hoofs, then the back, then the neck. Then the skinning begins. When he starts cutting into the animal, everyone asks the Creator for forgiveness for cutting into this carcass — for cutting into the meat of the deer and the skin as well. And when he cuts into the heart, they ask the Creator for an abundance of deer in the future.

In times past, there were no restrictions on killing deer. You were allowed to kill not only bucks but does as well, because they have a specific purpose in life. In other words, everything goes in two's — the male and the female. Nowadays, however, there are restrictions in all but a few areas, so that you are allowed to bring home only a buck. Some hunters go as far as 250 miles in order to reach an area where they can kill both a buck and doe, and this is a big moment for them.

As soon as the deer has been cleaned, a small bed is made on the east side of an evergreen tree or a cedar, or whatever nearby is green, and everything from the deer's insides is placed on this soft bed. Prayers are offered once again and charm stones are laid. And any animal that may be served as a result of the luck is invited to enjoy this dinner. Everyone then lends a hand in taking the deer back to camp. Once they reach camp, not a single piece of meat is touched; the men wait to arrive home.

At home in the meantime, people are going through their regular evening religious activities. All the children go out and pray to the Supreme God, and to the moon and stars, to protect the hunters and the wildlife. The grandfolks do the singing and the kids follow along, hoping that the hunters will appear any minute from above those hills. They do this for a period of four days and usually within those four days the hunters return — it's usually that quick. As the hunters approach, they start to build big fires so that the people in the village will know they are on their way. And when those back home see the fires — well, everybody, especially the kids, runs out to the hills to greet them, while the old folks offer prayers and sing and prepare for their arrival. They sweep the area where they will lay the deer and spread out a blanket and the things that are of value to them, like silver belts and moccasins.

Upon arrival, the hunters bring in the deer and lay it in a northerly direction. All the valuables are placed on it and the singing begins, and all the neighbors come and join in. If the hunters have been away for quite a long time and have therefore had a chance to cut a deer up and start drying its meat out in the open, they bring this meat along with them and lay it out. They cut a piece of it and give it to the people who are coming to join them — everybody who comes to this gathering gets a piece of meat.

Within four days, or later in the year when it's convenient, we have what we call a deer supper, and everybody in the village is invited. All during the month of November, for example, you can go from one deer dinner to another — everybody's invited. There is a great deal of preparation that goes into these dinners, and it gives you a wonderful feeling that there is this togetherness at home. As we go from dinner to dinner to eat, the old folks have a chance to give us advice; it gives them a chance to talk to us about life's way. These are quite some occasions, therefore. And, of course, every bit of deer meat is used, from the hoof on up to the tip of the horn. The one who made the kill has godparents and these parents are the ones who are the honored guests. They get the best part of the meat, which is usually from the head area.

When the meal is over, you don't just throw out the bones. All these bones are gathered and put in a basket along with other things that go with them. They are then taken to the nearest river or creek — in my case, it would be the San Jose River — and are dumped in, where they will eventually return to Mother Earth, and become the source of more life and sustenance. After these dinners, we have what we call a deer dance. The dancers wear our traditional dress, but in addition they put horns on their heads. People look forward to it and really enjoy it. In fact, nowadays people travel quite a distance, even from Zuni or from Taos, just to see this particular dance.

So this is the way we try to show our respect for the deer that provide us with food and clothing. Much of our clothing — our leggings, our moccasins, and so on, are made from deer hide, and most of the dyes we use come from the barks of various trees. Some are red, others are orange or yellow or brown. You have to pick the color you want, and know which tree to go to.

The hunt and the ceremonies connected with it are part of the teaching that children receive. They are taught how to behave in ceremonies like these. They are taught that they have to behave with a certain amount of restraint, and that they can't just run wild. During the ceremonies when something such as skinning is going on, they are also taught respect for animals. And they are taught patience. When you are hunting, they are told, you must not shoot at just anything that moves. You have to realize that you are out only to hunt deer. You might be walking along, for example, and all of a sudden a great big jack rabbit jumps up. You don't shoot at it, because you are out there for only one purpose. Even if you saw a bear, you wouldn't bother it, because you are prepared to hunt deer and that's all. And you are not there to hunt the deer with the biggest antlers. When I go hunting every now and then, I may see an eagle sitting up on one of those trees, and, golly, I've been wanting an eagle for all these many years! Now's my chance; but I just can't shoot it, because of what I've been taught. So a lot of teaching and discipline is involved and behavior patterns are established. You don't learn all of this in a matter of a few years. Sometimes it takes a lifetime just to remember it; but as you go along, you begin to understand the reason behind it.

MAX HANLEY: Sheep is the chief meat for the Navajo people. I started herding sheep when I was five years old — just a little bitty fellow, until I entered school when I was 8. I enrolled when I was 8 and I was so happy about it — they chopped all my hair off and my earrings, and cleaned me up. But in my younger days before that happened, I had quite a bit of experience with sheep. When you herd sheep, you always have dogs that go along with you. You have to name each dog and then tell them what to do in case the sheep scatter all over the area. There's some rough country where I come from, especially when you're by yourself. So you tell a certain dog: "Go over there and chase those sheep back, then run over there and bring in those other sheep." I usually had three dogs, and once in a while four.

My father, my mother and my grandfathers used to tell us what to do with the sheep. Suppose there are two people who go to look after them. One will stay on one side and the other on the other side, and the dog will walk all around so the coyote won't bother the sheep. If you don't watch out for him, old coyote will grab your little lambs and run away, and you can't catch him. In those days, we used to have some wolves, too. That wolf is quite dangerous. We used to live right close to the mountain, and once in a while the mountain lion would also come down to the desert. And sometimes the bear comes down, too, and kills the sheep, and gets some cattle. Now the government says that if these wolves and mountain lions and bears bother you, don't hesitate to kill them. But my grandfathers and my grandmother said, "You have to respect

them and leave them alone. They may be hungry, with nothing
to eat in their mouths. We have a lot of old sheep and crippled
sheep and so forth out there with the rest of the flock, so just
let them go. Let the bear or wolf have them. But the coyotes
always come after the lambs. They're the only ones you've got
to dispose of. If you've got a gun, kill them." All of this was
part of our early training. We were trained exactly the way kids
were brought up in the old days.

When we killed sheep for meat, we cut their throat. You
have to tie them up — all four quarters together — then cut their
throat and let them bleed for a while. That's the only thing I
sure hate to do. I usually let somebody else do it for me; but if
nobody is around, I have to do it myself. I close my eyes and
cut the throat and let all the blood run out. Then I pull the
head back and cut the spinal cord. I cut all the way down the
spine, take all the skin off, clean out the inside and clean the
inside of what they call the twisters, which are the intestines.
My grandchildren like these twisters. They always ask me,
"Grandpop, when are you going to get some more twisters?"

Just like Vic described, my uncles and grandfathers used to
go into the mountains with bows and arrows to hunt deer.
During the Civil War, some used a kind of long gun, and a few
years later we got new guns that were used during the First
World War and were better. What they were looking for was a
big buck with maybe three or four pointers. The main thing
they wanted it for was the skin. If you get a big buck with three
or four pointers, you will have nice thick skin that will last a
long time. The fewer the pointers, the thinner the skin.

Like the Pueblos, the Navajos are very careful about how
they treat the deer. Suppose you make a kill somewhere in the
mountains. You get ahold of its jaw and one of its front legs
and turn the deer around so that its head is close to your camp.
If you have white corn and black corn, you sprinkle them over
the deer.

The deer go to sleep between 11:00 in the morning until
2:00 or 2:30 in the afternoon, then they start to graze again.
Sometimes you may see a deer sleeping, maybe a big buck,
maybe a fawn; but if you find the doe you don't kill it, you let
it sleep. A deer that is lying down may see you before you see

it. Then it jumps out and makes a sound — SHHHH. Boy, they really scare you! They jump way up high and start running. When the big buck jumps up, you get so scared you don't know where you're shooting. You shoot anywhere. Sometimes you hit it if you're brave enough, but somehow those big bucks always scare you, no matter how brave you are.

ALLEN QUETONE: When we were young, it was hard to restrain us. They used to tell us certain things that we could and couldn't do, or should and shouldn't do when we were kids. Even so, we wanted to play and do things other than what we were told. If I had to stay all day long and watch sheep, I don't know what would have kept me there. How did they teach you to have the patience? What kind of training did you get? If it were me, I might be able to stand it for half a day, but then I'd want to run down to the creek or the river and take a swim.

MAX HANLEY: This is what happened. My grandfather and grandmother used to tell me, "You have to take care of your sheep all day long." Of course, I didn't have any sandwiches then — no turkey sandwich, nothing — just corn, that's all. And I carried a little water with me in a jug-like container. I had to go out around noon, and I stayed out there with the sheep, maybe in a shady place, and let them rest. I might go to sleep, too, but not for long. Otherwise the sheep

would stray away and be chased all over by the coyote or wolf. So I had to stay with them and keep a good lookout, especially for the coyote that comes around to kill the lambs. Sometimes they don't even eat them, they just kill. You see some lambs just lying about with chewed throats. That's the reason you stay around and look out for them. And if you don't, grandfather will get after you and whip you for it. You're sure to get a whipping. Just like in the morning. Grandfather would come around and say, "Hey grandson! Get up!" Maybe you don't

MAX HANLEY — Navajo

hear him. Next time he comes around and you're still in bed, he
gets the double rope and, boy, he almost hits you — he just
barely shaves you. But you can feel it and it makes you jump!
That's how they put pressure on you.

ALLEN QUETONE: I have always heard that the
Southwest tribes have a great deal of patience, and I think this
adds up, because of their way of life. They are a quiet and
peaceful people, and I think these qualities are overriding in
their total behavior. You can still see it. All you have to do is go
to Navajo country. There is a difference in the way they behave.
I guess you could call it a quiet, still strength because the
Navajos today are very strong people, strong in their own
traditions. And they intend to stay this way.

HENRY OLD COYOTE: The Crows are taught that
everything you see has a purpose in this world and contributes
something to life. There is a purpose behind everything; there is
a force out there and that same force is responsible for all that
surrounds you. This applies even to hunting. We are taught that
if we go hunting and get some meat, we leave a little for the
flesh-eating animals and birds that are out there. We usually
address everything in general that we've left this meat so that all
the flesh-eating animals can share it with us. By doing this, we
hope to continue to have good luck on our hunting expeditions.
If we are fortunate enough to have food that is a little better
than what we are used to, we are thankful and share it even
with pets. We will also take a piece of it and put it in the river,
put it in the fire; so we are sharing with the river and the fire.
When a person is in mourning or feels bad, he forgets about
building a fire and the fire goes out. So when we put that piece
of meat in the fire, we are asking the fire not to go out; in other
words, we don't want bad luck to come into our homes.

It has been a popular belief that Indians go out and
worship animals and birds. I believe the dominant society has
the wrong impression, because this is a misinterpretation. The
Indians more or less used the animals as symbols in their
religious ceremonies or when offering thanks. Take the buffalo.
The buffalo was the livelihood of the Plains Indian. From it he
got his clothing, his food, his tools and his home. In paying
tribute to it, he used the buffalo head in the ceremony as a

symbol, a reminder of what this animal contributed to his life. That is why the Plains Indian respects and pays tribute to the buffalo. There are various parts of other animals, or pictures or images of these animals and birds, that you may see on an Indian's clothing or costume. They are worn as reminders that these animals play a part in our life.

We are taught always to respect our surroundings. For example, different clans take different things as their patrons. The one my wife belongs to is known as the Greasy Mouth. The Greasy Mouths take the sun as a patron. They are the ones who rise with the sun. They're not actually sun worshippers, but they respect the sun and address it as Old Man; in turn, they are the ones who can communicate with the sun. Then there are others who take birds as their patrons. So they rise with the birds. In the early morning the birds are happy. They are singing and making music, so if you rise with the birds and join in the rejoicing of the new day, you are going to be lucky that day. You are going to be healthy that day. This is their belief.

There are also clans that take different animals as patrons and have celebrations either by themselves or with others when these animals have young ones in spring. The Indian New Year is when everything reproduces, when everything freshens all over and little birds start having young ones. The earth, the world, is reproducing right at that time. That's when certain clans want to pay tribute to the new freshness of spring.

As I mentioned, we think of the moon as the Grandmother and the sun as the Old Man. The sun has been here ever since man can remember, so he must be very old; therefore he's an Old Man. When you see a new day you see the Old Man coming up over the horizon. There are many misconceptions about the Indian addressing the moon and the sun in this way. We are called moon-worshippers and sun-worshippers. But we don't actually worship the sun; we simply appreciate the fact that the sun is there. We worship whoever is responsible for that sun coming up over the horizon. You often see pictures or paintings of an Indian raising his hands in supplication. A lot of people don't understand why an Indian gets into that position. Well, what he's doing is going out alone and giving thanks to those forces out there, those forces that bring him so many good things in life.

13

THE MAGIC MISSION
OF THE AMERICAN INDIAN

SYLVESTER MOREY: The references all of you have
made to the Indian's profound gratitude to nature and his
respect for the spirit that comes to expression in nature
reminds me of the first proposed topic for this conference —
magic. Magic not in the sense of Mandrake the Magician, but
from a spiritual point of view. The idea was suggested by the
late Dr. Franz Winkler, former President of the Myrin Institute,
at a luncheon meeting with Commissioner Bruce, Allen Quetone
and myself in Washington, D.C. Certain of the things that have
been said at this conference could just as well have been said if
we were discussing magic. I'd like to refer to some shorthand
notes that were taken at that meeting, because I think they
emphasize the importance of the traditional Indian approach to
life and suggest how this approach could help both Indian and
non-Indian. Keep in mind that our word, 'magic,' comes from a
Persian word that originally meant 'the power of wisdom.' Dr.
Winkler observed: "Magic follows a definite relationship
between inner and outer elements or forces. Under the Indian
concept, man can affect nature. If the tribe needs rain, its
longing for rain, if purified or strengthened, brings rain. If you
become sufficiently aware of inner water, you will be aware of
the influence it has on outer water or nature. We are composed
predominantly of water. This means that the essence of the

water forces is in us. The Indian could stimulate the water organism both within and without. Magic resides in understanding this connection between the inner and the outer.

"In the past, magic existed everywhere. Eventually, people changed the proper use of magic into a selfish craving to achieve concrete things. Thus they developed great external power, but they lost magic. (We are not speaking of magic in the trivial sense, but in the sense of man's direct connection with spiritual forces.) This was the beginning of the decline of various civilizations. Most nations have been in decline for so long that no magic remains as spiritual substance in them. Under the impact of modern education, which does away with magic completely, young people have no dreams left. Dreams are magic. What should be dreams leading to creative enthusiasm has given way to a tedious, moralistic exercise in duty. This is one reason why young poople no longer wish to participate in the 'establishment' — particularly the established white culture.

"If we speak of the East Indians, we can understand why American youth today is drawn to them. It is because they have the most impressive history of magic. Egypt, on the other hand, lost her magic hundreds and hundreds of years ago. But there are American Indians who are still to some extent living in a world of magic. The real reason young Indians become militant once they are taken away from tribal lore and ritual practices is that they are lost, frustrated, and angry when cut off from magic dreams and magic power. If one could save the magic still alive in the traditional Indian ways and translate it into modern concepts and practices, one could save the world. The young of the world are looking for any kind of leadership that will make life livable.

"There are three areas of magic: the magic in man's relationship to nature; the magic in his relationship to his fellowman; the magic in his relationship to God. The last is magic in its purest form: that is, when you know the Great Spirit is everywhere and you depend on him for everything you want to achieve. Regardless of the area, all true magic lies in the sacred use of will power.

"When magic is misused, it becomes so-called 'black

magic.' Black magic is a real sin, because in it man violates what is sacred. To misuse the Holy Spirit is to commit the worst sin. But people long for the spirit, and if they cannot find it to their salvation through white magic, they will look for it to their destruction in black magic.

"To translate the forces of white magic into a modern form would be the saving of our nation. The white race wants it very much now. But it has been too long since we lost our knowledge of magic. The Indian still retains a feeling for this spiritual power. The magic mission of the American Indian was to develop the sacred use of will power. The hippies who have turned to Indian traditions have too little will. This is why so many hippies are attracted to Indians. They feel the Indian will power, which they lack. White people have completely lost the sense for how to train will power.

"Indians have a great deal of will power training, but very little intellectual training. The Indians instinctively knew that intellect in certain ways subdues magic, and they did not want this to happen. Intellect, nevertheless, has to be trained, just as does will power. To use the intellectual training of the white race, but put it on an equal footing with will power training as it existed in the old Indian traditions, would develop complete human beings. Imagine what it would be like if we could bring up young people so that they could endure pain, if necessary, the way the Indians did! Although the Indians' emotions were strong, they were not permitted to become either hysterical or sentimental. How can our young people today be educated so that they are emotionally strong? It can only be done by training their will power, on the one hand, and on the other their intellect, to such a degree that between the two, in the heart, they are able to feel with stronger, deeper emotions: so that real courage, real tenderness, real love develop.

"Every part of life, every turning point in life, requires the magic of blessing. The child still lives in a magic world, but when he enters adolescence he needs strong medicine to make the right transition from childhood to puberty. So many children lose themselves at puberty because life's magic is gone. If you suddenly become adult without really growing up — as generally happens today to both men and women — you get childish actions in sex. The young person approaching adolescence needs someone to tell him, 'Now you are going into a new phase. You have to look at life in a new way.'

"*Every* phase in life has to have its memorable, deeply significant celebration. How, for example, can one explain to young people that they should undergo and remain faithful to a marriage whose ceremony has come to mean almost nothing? It is difficult to give up one's freedom and live with another person in marriage; unless the original ceremony has had true magic to inspire, to set the foundation for this event, it may become impossible. Such magic involves stern discipline as well as the sense of wonder and awe."

ALLEN QUETONE: Dr. Winkler, I believe, was using the word 'magic' in its broadest sense: to mean the mystery, the spirit, of what Indian people believe. In other words, magic, as he used it, has to do with this thing we've talked about for the last few days — this unseen power, this spirit that surrounds us and that we know is there. We respect it; we live by it.

JOHN GARDNER: The white man has not always lacked closeness to that Great Spirit, or understanding of the sacred ceremonies, rituals and reverence that lead to him. Only just now we whites are in very short supply of these things: not because we are white but because of a certain kind of thinking that has become predominant among us.

Unfortunately, a farmer today would think it a big waste of time to go through some ceremony or other before he plows the earth. He doesn't believe his attitude makes any difference when he puts in the grain. He thinks it makes no difference whether the seed comes out of his hands or whether it comes out of a mechanical seeder. He thinks it is all the same however he looks over his crop, and with what thoughts he works it, with what thoughts he harvests and mills it. A doctor thinks it makes no difference, once he has certain substances in hand, just how, with what thoughts and feelings, he puts them together and dispenses them as medicine. He believes there is nothing more to medicine than chemistry. A person, on the other hand, who believes a little more in the magic of life feels that a doctor with a very good heart may have a different effect with that same medicine than a doctor without much heart.

What we are talking about is the power that prevails over all and works through a good man if he prays, if he prepares himself. For example, all of your traditions show that a man must be purified if he is to become a proper instrument for the higher power. When Dr. Winkler was speaking of the possibility of bringing magic into life, I believe he had in mind people who wished to be of service, who wished to bring to others the beauty and grace of the spirit. All of life should be filled with this force, this spiritual grace, so that the parent gives a real blessing to his child, the mother to the father, the father to the mother, man to nature, and all of the elements to man. There should be the give and take of spiritual power. But now in our times, we have become egotists and everybody pushes his own power as far as he can. Few of us are pure conduits for the higher power. Dr. Winkler claimed that we long, nonetheless, to feel ourselves in touch with something beyond ourselves; and he stressed that when people cannot bring this about in a good way, they will do it in a bad way.

SYLVESTER MOREY: Magic is also the ability to communicate with the inner spirit of another being, whether it be a plant or animal or man; it is the ability to read the signs of nature in the sense in which some of you were speaking earlier.

ALLEN QUETONE: Let me give you my impression of Dr. Winkler, strictly from a feeling standpoint. As far as I am concerned, I have never met a white man who had the intuitive understanding Dr. Winkler had about Indian thinking and Indian attitudes. Talking to him was just like talking to another Indian. Somehow another Indian knows, often without saying anything, that he is reaching a person and communicating. This was the feeling I had with Dr. Winkler. I knew he understood me.

HENRY OLD COYOTE: I call it the built-in radar system to each other.

VICTOR SARRACINO: I would like to raise a question, if I may. Suppose there is an individual who is capable of having forces work through him. Does it mean that he can only perform a certain thing when he happens to fall in line with that mystical force, that he can have this wisdom and good magic one day but may not have it the next day? All around him is the White Spirit; but there are black forces, too. How do you distinguish between them, and which one gains the upper hand?

JOHN GARDNER: The way I look at it, life itself, ordinary life, is very often a battle. What Victor raises is an important point, because we are talking about active forces here, not just abstractions. In modern times, we don't have to face grizzly bears very often, unless we take a plane and go into the wilds looking for one. We seldom have to face natural disasters, because we are so protected; as a rule, we don't even have to face extreme heat or cold. Thus people have lost all sense of the heroic. We don't know what the challenge of life is any more. The hunt is no longer a vital part; people no longer idealize war. So we come to one of the biggest questions modern man faces: what is it in our present civilization that can challenge the human spirit and bring out what is manly and strong in it? What gives us the sense of adventure and makes us fully alert? What makes it possible for us to develop courage, endurance and watchfulness as traditional Indians once did?

It seems to me that in our time there isn't much point to life, unless people become aware that we are *always* living in a battlefield of forces, good and bad, that these forces are real, and that although they are greater than man, they can and must be influenced by human action and will power. I believe this is the way things actually are. We are always just in the intersection between good and bad possibilities, and these possibilities are perhaps more real today than ever before. If you become aware of this fact, you will know why it is so important to have a modern equivalent of the traditional rites of purification: sweat houses, fasting, isolation, prayers, and so on — and on the other side, why you would want to undergo exercises to strengthen your will: through trials of patience, courage, endurance, and the like. We should understand the point of the old ceremonies: that they help a man to perfect himself through the training and discipline they afford, so that he can be of service to the good and capable of fighting the bad. And there is plenty of bad to fight. I'm not talking now about the evil in witchery, black magic, and so on. I'm talking about much of modern civilization, which is itself bewitched and not a good thing, either for man or for nature.

SYLVESTER MOREY: I would like to add one word in answer to Victor's questions about where black forces and white forces meet. They meet in the soul of every human being, and it is the free will of every human being to choose between them. The reason there is black magic is to help you develop strength. If you weren't subjected to temptation, there would be no way for you to develop inner strength. Suppose everything always went beautifully and you always did the right thing: you would not be a strong person. A strong person is a person who has been able to resist temptation.

JOHN GARDNER: It is the heart, I think, that distinguishes between black and white forces. We awaken the heart when we try to become aware of what is hidden in life. The effort to gain a clear perception of just what Vic is talking about — where good and evil meet in man — is probably the greatest challenge of our time. It is by purifying yourself that you protect yourself against the influence of evil forces. You battle against and overcome what you have recognized as evil; you drive it from your soul.

Dr. Winkler, I believe, wanted to bring up as strange a subject as magic, which has such a doubtful sound to it, and have a whole conference about it, because he felt it was necessary to look at things from the point of view of the mystery, the creative power for good, that lies within them. Only then are we able to see and resist evil when it draws near, and to open our hearts fully to the power of the good.

14

THE MODERN INDIAN'S DILEMMA

ALLEN QUETONE: Because of his exposure to the dominant society, the American Indian has suffered the breakdown of his culture and of the things he held dear. He was happy, he was in harmony with his environment and with the world. This happiness was broken down, although we still have remnants of it. The Indian people had great respect for God or Spirit, but this belief is also gradually losing its influence.

Our discussions have been an attempt to relate from our own experiences some of the old ways the Indians taught their young in the various stages of their growth. We have tried to consider the Indian's religion, the way he regarded the world around him, his relation to his fellow man. In other words, we have focused on things that were basic in his life and are basic to the life of all human beings, because all of us agree that there was much in the traditional Indian's life from which we could benefit today.

While we believe these traditional ways could serve as guidelines for our future and bring us happiness, we face great frustrations. Our ways seem always to contradict the ways of the dominant society. We find hardship in trying to be Indian and true to our beliefs and at the same time trying to survive in the mainstream of modern life. Let me show you what I mean.

In the Indian way of life, the traditional life, there was a time for growing up. At each stage of life, there was no rushing; you did not skip. You had to go from this stage to the next one and on to the next one, and there was no way of getting around it. There was no short cut.

Today, with such emphasis on education — and I think Indian children are going through the same thing as non-Indian children — there is a strong push to get your child in the pre-primary, primary and first grades and start him off reading and doing things that are actually beyond his years. He is rushed through the different stages of his childhood. The Indians feel that each stage is crucial and that the child should be allowed to dwell in each for the appropriate period of time so that every aspect of his being can evolve, just as a plant evolves in the proper time and sequence of the seasons. Otherwise, the child never has a chance to master himself in any one phase of his life. Nowadays, however, we live under constant pressure. I don't know where it comes from, but there is a constant push; and if you don't conform, you are out.

Already when I was a boy, there was a constant pressure to go off to school, to cut your hair, to be as non-Indian as you possibly could. This pressure was on you; it was forced on you. So eventually the white method of teaching began to catch on, because even Indian children were beginning to take hold of white standards. At least this happened in the school I was in. Indian kids were making fun of other Indian kids because they didn't speak properly, or because they didn't dress properly. These standards were thrust upon them and were finally accepted. This went on until right after World War II, when there was a complete reversal because the returning veterans had seen what was going on in the rest of the world. They began to realize that there was never anything wrong with their way of life in the first place; that it should not have been put down as it was by trying to change Indians through government action. All of us are probably victims, in a sense, of this early trend of federal education, and it affected our total Indian outlook, and our rituals and traditions.

To make a further point: right after the War, the traditional Indian world was just about at a standstill. You could see it happen in my home territory, because on the east side of the state we have the Five Civilized tribes that are a hundred years ahead of us in terms of mimicking the non-Indian world. You could always tell the difference where Five Civilized Tribes kids and Western Oklahoma kids went to the same school. They were already saying and doing things that the Western Oklahoma Indians were not fully aware of. So they set a standard. In other words, "Boy, if you don't do this . . . ." It was the same kind of stuff that happens in schools today. They were further ahead, and it made our kids want to be like them, which again was the problem of conflicting standards. I merely mention this to show that I think a lot of these things were responsible for the breakdown of many of our beautiful traditions.

VICTOR SARRACINO: What Allen is saying reminds me of an incident in my own youth. I had a cousin with whom I grew up until his family moved to a city in Arizona. He and I used to discuss Indian leaders, bows and arrows, and all that stuff. Six months after he'd moved, he came back for a visit and he talked about nothing except bad men and robbing and Tonto and the Lone Ranger. He struck me as kind of funny. I was listening to him and he said, "I think Lone Ranger can beat your chief up." He had that kind of thinking in just six months' time! And he talked about Hitler and what Hitler did. He'd use a gun and I'd use a bow and arrow when we'd go out into the hills and play war. It was quite a change.

JIMMY BEGAY: In my case, I have to wear two hats. Both my parents are real traditional. They have no formal schooling. I guess Dad is the same as Max is. My Mom is the mother of the whole household and Dad takes care of the chores. That's the way it goes. We listen mostly to our mother about everything Navajo, particularly where discipline is concerned. Most of my speech is in Navajo at home, and I have

JIMMY BEGAY — Navajo

to relate everything in Navajo to my parents. I would say that our culture is about 85% strong, and I seem to cling more to the Navajo side, though I have been exposed to the white world through my schooling and my work. As I say, I have to wear two hats. That's the way it is now and I guess it will have to remain that way for the rest of my life.

JOHN GARDNER: Throughout our discussions we have touched upon the contradictions between white and Indian ways. The Indian attitudes toward discipline and obedience, toward parents and grandparents, toward sex, toward nature, are often the opposite of what many modern white educators, psychiatrists and technicians advocate. From what do these differences stem? Unless we clearly understand what the dilemma of the modern Indian consists of and just where it lies, we will never even approach a workable solution to it, or find a set of values that could benefit the non-Indian as well.

ALLEN QUETONE: Indian people have a very difficult time conforming to the system and to the institutions that prevail in the country, because they are creatures of individual freedom. It goes against their nature to conform to abstract systems and to formalized rules and regulations that have no objective reality to them. It took me quite a while to figure out why the white man conforms to systems so easily . After much deliberation, I finally came to this conclusion:

Since earliest times, white people have had kings. They have had leaders, and this custom has developed over hundreds and hundreds of years. The rulers owned everything; people lived under them at their whim. The rulers ruled, they made the laws, they set the standards. For centuries you have had people living under this type of system. After a time, Columbus crossed the ocean; with him came great numbers of people who had lived under this system. They set up towns, they set up rules. They met a strange people who shot bows and arrows, who had a way of living together with mutual respect for each other, without arbitrary classes of society, and with leaders who were clearly the outstanding members of the tribe. I accept the explanation of the influence of the Iroquois Confederacy on the forming of the Constitution and the first government of the settlers. The fact that there might be some contribution by Indians to the ideas expressed in the Constitution is logical and reasonable and is supported by the heritage of both cultures.

Taking into account the existence of rulers and kings in the white man's past before he came to America (and how this continued to color his idea of freedom), gave me a better understanding of why I am different from white people. I don't have this same long background. I have mine in something else, although there are times when I don't agree with this Indian way of being an individual. We have a hard time agreeing in council meetings. Everybody has to have his say; every man has this right. We may have a very important decision to make. It may take six months, or it may take a year; but that decision is not going to be made until everyone has his say and the issue goes around and is fully discussed. We respect the right of each individual.

This reminds me of something else. No talk is ever given without first indicating your humility. "I am an ignorant man; I am a poor man" − all the talks start this way − "I don't know nearly as much as you men sitting around here, but I would like to express my humble opinion," and then he'll knock you down with logic and wisdom.

But these are the things that give me a better understanding of the white man's ways. I can better appreciate why white people conform so easily. There are books written today saying that we are all becoming robots; all we have to do is hear a bell and we automatically do something. We run for the door or jump in our cars to rush some place. Indians don't do this yet, and this is one reason why they don't make good workers − at least this is what businessmen say.

Down where I live, we are discussing the possibility of using retired businessmen for job training of certain Indians. We've met with some of these men and asked them openly, "Why don't you hire Indians?" They are reluctant, of course. They don't want to say things in front of you that might be offensive, but they point out that you have to get work out between eight and five o'clock, that you have to be there on time because this machine has to start and you have to produce. And an Indian − he may not wake up; he may have visited late

the night before or gone to a powwow, and he comes in at ten
o'clock. These kinds of problems, of not conforming to the
system, mean that we are constantly torn between two things. I
think it's good that we are talking about ways to have one foot
over here and the other foot over there. We Indians have to do
both properly — I guess that's the key. So you can see that in
addition to problems of education, the Indians have a problem
fitting into society as it exists today.

HENRY OLD COYOTE: You know by the responsibilities
given to certain individuals that the elders feel: "Here is a man
who can be depended on, whom we can entrust with rites." But
he's employed by a white man, and at a certain time — I'm
talking about the moons and things like that — the Indians want
to perform a ceremony and it doesn't happen to fall on Sunday,
the fourth of July, or Christmas. When the conditions are just
right it falls on a working day. This Indian is torn between his
job and his responsibility to his people. So he goes to the
ceremony and the white employer says, "That Indian is
unreliable." But where he is being depended upon by his own
people, he's a reliable man. So that is why I suggested at one
time that they set aside an "Indian Christmas" and an "Indian
Easter" and have it a flexible date, like your Easter.

Another point I would like to make is that we have respect
for certain things. Take a biology class. The Indian student will
refrain from dissecting certain little creatures, and the teacher
therefore gives him a poor grade for not participating. He may
have a reason for not participating, but the teacher doesn't
bother to find out why. He just gives the student a poor grade.
The student may have reasons because of his background; he
may have a respect that forbids him to do the things the others
are doing.

I knew of some boys who were taking a biology class. One
boy had skinned his arm, and rather than cutting into an
animal, he would break his own scab and take the blood. He
would rather take it from his own body than dissect that poor
little frog over there.

VICTOR SARRACINO: There are many of our young
boys who are left out of athletic activities at home around
Pueblo. Around the basketball and football season, many of the

Pueblos have these religious activities going, where they are not supposed to cut their hair. So they make a choice. They either have their hair cut to play ball, or stay home and go through this ritual. Some don't have an opportunity to go on to college. Then they remain at home, and go to be initiated. Many times they say, "I wish that I could play basketball with my long hair, but the coach says no." To me it's not a real crime for a guy to play with long hair, and this attitude seems to be gaining acceptance now.

ALLEN QUETONE: Last night Henry told us about Earl Old Person who used to play basketball with braids. Earl, a Blackfoot, is past President of the National Congress of American Indians. He was the Blackfoot Tribal Council Chairman, but I never knew about this basketball prowess. When he fought for the ball underneath the basket, he would throw his braids around. Apparently, the athletic council passed a rule that you could no longer play with braids. Secret weapon!

HENRY OLD COYOTE: When they had the Boy Scout World Jamboree in Europe, he was the representative from this area. As a boy, before he entered politics, he was a Boy Scout and he had braids. Even in school he had long hair, but then he had to cut his hair because of age and because he was in the state legislature. He became noted as the first Indian who attended that Boy Scout World Jamboree in Europe.

ERNEST BENEDICT: In my case, I was pretty well frustrated as a child. I didn't know what was going on, really. You have a church that influences children at a fairly early age. Some kids go to Sunday School when they are about four years old — pre-kindergarten. One of the things they learn is that there should be love and affection one for another, and of course most Indian children do receive this at home. But if they don't learn a lesson very well, they are spanked in Sunday School. They can't understand that; they don't get spanked at home.

We used to be told, "You are going to have to go to school to learn to help your people." I was forced to travel 300 miles away from home to attend a school that would teach me something that would be helpful to my people. But my people were back there; they were 300 miles back home!

Another thing. They teach us how great men will serve *their people.* Then they teach us how to get a skill that will get us a good job that will eventually lead to an even higher paying job or launch us into some field that will glorify us *personally.* There are a whole lot of things that just don't add up. These things are contradictory and I'm afraid that because of them there are dropouts not only from school but from society. Alcoholism, of course, is a big thing, and the suicide rate has gone up in the past ten years. Homes are pretty well breaking up, and even those that are staying together cannot always be happy. We're in a great turmoil.

I think young people now are trying to reason a way out of this. I think they are turning to traditional things; but the people the young Mohawks are turning to — people who are 70 and 80 years old — unfortunately are the ones who were the prime targets of the missionary efforts of two generations ago and of the schooling and other exploitation that occurred. These people moved outside of the reservations, and some of them moved for perhaps a whole generation. Then when they got very old, they brought their families back to the reservation. But then the families didn't have any of the language or traditions of their people. So they slowly had to rebuild some of these old customs and gain respect for them again. A number of other tribes have come into the reservation from various parts of Canada and New England. The Micmacs originally were pushed out of Maine and then roamed through the New England states. They went up into southern Quebec for a while and then were routed from there. Eventually, three groups came to our reservation for refuge and were taken in. Their own traditions, as far as we can tell, are forgotten, and they took up the Mohawk language and were adopted into the Mohawk tribe.

My own father's family through the male line were Micmacs; and so, from the Micmac side, my family has been pretty short and stocky. That perhaps explains my own size compared to other Mohawks, who are usually quite tall.

The Mohawks have retained very little of the real authentic Indian. There may be a few things we can point to and say we have kept: a knowledge of medicines, the clan structure, family structure, names, but much of this is fragmented. It's all in little pockets. It is very hard to find anyone who is actually a Mohawk Indian and knows all of the traditions of his people, and all the reasons behind them. Of course, our big concern, and the thing we are holding onto very desperately, is our concept of political life and political thought. This, I believe, is something that we have been able to retain: the idea of being part of a group and not just individuals. So we have kept some of our traditions in spite of everything, but we have had to sacrifice a great deal for this.

ERNEST BENEDICT —
Mohawk

Many of the younger people don't even know what clan they belong to. But now they have discovered that there are such things as clans, and they want to be identified by their clan; they want to be known by the name that belongs to their clan. Some of them never even had an Indian name. So things are beginning to change.

The younger Indians are becoming more interested in their background and are insisting that the elders of the tribe tell them just what is true. Now they have books to go to and they are checking up on the older people. Even in my lifetime, there are quite a few 'traditions' that seem to have sprung up as instant traditions. When one of the elders got stuck and couldn't remember what the old tradition was, he invented one on the spot, and some of them are pretty ridiculous. These are being picked over by the young people who are learning what it is all about. So they are insisting that the information be authentic; and if there is no surviving tradition, then they are going to members of other tribes and asking them about some of theirs.

As far as I know, the Iroquois traditions are almost 100% gone, but we are slowly rediscovering them. St. Regis is part of the Mohawk nation, which in turn is part of the Iroquois family. At one time the Iroquois were known as the Five Nations, which is a political grouping; it also represents a group of languages. Most of the Iroquois belong to the Five Nations Confederacy, but not all of them. The Hurons, who were a related group, did not join the Five Nations Confederacy and in fact were considered enemies and eventually lost their tribal identity, so that there are very few Hurons left. A few who call themselves Hurons have a reservation near Quebec City, but they are very much mixed with white blood.

ALLEN QUETONE: Probably all the Indian kids across the country are going through the same thing. There is a sudden awareness of being Indian, and everybody is going back, or at least making a grand search for some identity and some tie-in with traditionalism. The college kids are grasping for some tie-in through their Indian studies programs. On the reservations, the kids are now trying to find more authentic information, more of their own traditions, and I think it must be very difficult, with so few elders who can give this kind of information.

ERNEST BENEDICT: Our young people are now exploring the significance of the old Iroquois village idea. It is well known that in early historical times the Iroquois had a whole number of palisaded villages through the center of New York State, where we are quite well identified with the old historical figures. So this idea that the village is a home base, that the men go off hunting and then come back to the village, is a tradition of our people. It survives today with the family being based on the reservation and with the men going off to earn a living in the cities — maybe as far away as New York City — and driving home on weekends to be with the family, and to bring back money that will bring food. This idea is spreading now to the younger people.

In the old days, the villages were very compact. There might be only one clan within that one village, and the next village, perhaps twenty miles or so away, might be composed of the people of another clan, so that the families or clans, because of this compactness, started to hold everything in common. Even the gardens would be kept as community gardens, and the people would go out and plant and work together. Some of the planting songs and planting ceremonies that were used when everybody held their gardens together are still preserved. Last summer some young people asked for and received garden space from some of the old people in our community. They planted and took care of it. It was kind of haphazard last year, but the crops were put into a common storehouse and people were invited to come and take what they wanted. Then some of the grain was ground up and flour was distributed. This year on the farm that I have, two gardens of about three acres were planted by the same young people. Quite a few have joined that group, so that now they are more numerous.

ALLEN QUETONE: I have tried to recreate a traditional atmosphere for my children, knowing that I am much away from home and knowing what they are exposed to at school. It may seem artificial, but I have tried in my own ways to combat this influence and to tell them we are Indian; and, of course, they know we are. At school they tell the other kids they're Indian, but the kids don't believe them. So they have to come home for proof.

To give a sense of reality to their Indianness, I tell the boys what I went through and what my grandparents did for me, and it works to this extent. I make it sound so adventurous that they would like to live the same way. So when we go home to Oklahoma, the first thing they want to do is to see their grandfather; they think that just as soon as they see their grandfather, they are going to experience the same thing I did, automatically. But the situation is not the same. There are no horses around; there are no creeks. The point is this: The appeal still exists today, but there is no physical environment for it.

VICTOR SARRACINO: When I traveled with my family in the northwestern area of the States, no matter where we went, I immediately enrolled my kids in school. A lot of people told me, "It's very difficult to enroll your kids when you're traveling; it's hard to find a place to stay." We never had that problem. We just went to a motel or hotel and they took us in. I think it was an amusement to these people, because it was a big family that came in. Anyway, when I enrolled my children, the other kids would immediately notice that these were Indians. They would ask, "Do you dance?" and we would say, "Of course we do." It was a lucky thing we had all our artifacts. So we made arrangements to dance at some of these schools and we got along real well. Of course, as influential as I was, we even got some of the teachers drumming, and we had the kids dancing! They really enjoyed it. Then when we got to the mountains, I took my kids out and showed them around. Even if I went into the city, I could still show my kids the same things I used to see as a child. I could drive out and go down to a creek or up into the mountains and show them the same things. It doesn't have to be artificial.

HENRY OLD COYOTE: I would like to remind some of the people here of a few things that deal with an Indian's identity. I was told that I was an Indian. I was told that I was a Crow Indian because I belonged to the Crow tribe. I also belong to a clan, which makes me eligible to be a member of the various societies that go along with it. The reason I am eligible for certain societies, certain rituals and certain offices is the simple fact that I was born a man; I am male.

Now, in the designs of the Indian people, in the jewelry, the hairdos and so on, a distinction is made between male and female, as well as between the various tribes. There are certain identifying marks. We have teenagers today who have lost their identity as Indians but want to regain it. So they take ornaments and wear them indiscriminately; they let their hair grow and don't take care of it. But the hairdo distinguishes the tribes. The Navajos have a certain hairdo; the Arapahos have a certain hairdo. In the northwest, some tribes wear just one braid, some wear three, and some wear the foretops. Then we have the distinguishing ornaments. If a little baby is born and it's a boy, someone will make a little moccasin that is kept next to the baby, signifying a long journey, expeditions, war parties, and what have you. If it's a little girl, someone may make an awl for use in piercing different hides. They may bead it and put it on the little girl so that anyone who sees her will know, "That baby is a girl." There is also a certain way of putting on red paint to show whether the child is a boy or girl. It is just like the aprons Dutch children wear; both boys and girls wear aprons, but the color distinguishes the sex of the child. It's similar to that.

What these teenagers do is take everything and mix it up without regard for the significance of the ornament. They want to say they are Indian, but a man will probably be wearing a woman's symbol, and all that. They don't care whether they are man or woman. You can't distinguish them — they are just 'Indians.' It kind of irks other people that this younger set has no respect for anything anymore. They know they are Indian, but they don't know what respect is.

Individuals from certain societies have certain amulets, and there is a proper way of wearing them, just as the knights used to wear heraldic devices signifying the household they were from, and the Scotsman his identifying kilt. The Indian wears the colors and designs of his tribe or clan and there is a certain way of wearing them. But the younger Indians today take these colors and symbols and wear them any which way.

How do we get through to these people? How do we approach them without insulting them, without rubbing them the wrong way, to tell them they are doing wrong? They take feathers and wear them any place. But there are certain ways of wearing feathers, as far as the older people are concerned. They abuse what the old people respect.

ALLEN QUETONE: Back in traditional times, one of the ways of keeping people in line was through community pressure. Today there is no Indian community pressure to keep young people in line. I feel insulted because many young Indians aren't taking enough interest in their background. Yet it's right within their grasp. Their fathers and their grandfathers are still around to give them information, but they are reluctant to take advantage of their knowledge. I don't know whether it is because of a lack of time or because they don't want to come under the influence of their elders. Regardless of what it is, it's there. The militant movements, which we have primarily in the urban areas, are to me the most flagrant abuse of Indian custom and philosophy, and involve people who should know better.

SYLVESTER MOREY: I think many young people have

not found a useful way of making themselves important, so they make themselves important by doing something that is not useful, is perhaps even destructive, but which attracts attention. They are trying to make themselves important in the wrong way, because they haven't found anything in life which they would like to do or from which they could derive lasting satisfaction.

VICTOR SARRACINO: It's interesting to observe the difference between young Indians who have stayed close to their roots and those who have left their families and homes and gone away to school or college. There's a kid who lives next door to me who is my nephew. He has lived on the reservation all his life and been involved in all kinds of traditions. He went to the high school on the reservation, where the Indian enrollment must be 95%. He's never worried about his identity, about whether or not he is an Indian.

He's at Western University now. During his second year, he became president of his fraternity. He still is, and next year he'll be a senior. For the past three years he's worked at IBM's Data Processing and his boss told me privately that when he finishes Western University, he will offer him a job as Assistant Vice President at IBM. Here's a kid who has never been outside the reservation, but who has just gone on with his studies.

On the other hand, a lot of his Indian friends at Western went away to public schools and lived in the city. Now they are having problems because they are trying hard to prove they are Indian. It has kept them away from their studies and their regular college work. My nephew has just stuck with his college work and has gone right on through. I've heard him say, "Some of my friends are in Indian clubs, Indian studies, and so on. I know all that. I just want to learn what I need to learn in college." You see, he didn't have to prove that he was Indian. That was the least of his worries, because he knew who he was all the time.

Those Indians who have gone away from their people know that they have left something behind. They discover the Indian values that they miss in Indian clubs and things like that, and when they come home, they continuously ask us about the traditional ways. They want to follow them; they want to know about them. In fact, not too long ago another nephew of mine was married out at one of the springs in an Indian ceremony. It was quite wonderful to see this and to realize that many young Indians who have been cut off from their people and their past are beginning to be interested in the old ways.

JOHN GARDNER: I would gather two things from what you have just said. On the one hand, the self-confidence of those Indians who have been cut off from their culture prematurely is weakened and undermined. They cannot find themselves in the white world, whose values are so contrary to their own, and yet they have not spent sufficient time in their own world, especially in the early years, to gather from it the strength they need. They are severed from those values that are their natural right, before their deeper identity, whose growth these values nourish, has matured. These Indians lack confidence and desperately seek to establish an identity through what you might call artificial means — through Indian clubs, Indian studies, Red power, etc. On the other hand, those Indians who have been allowed to mature within their culture, whose deeper sense of themselves develops naturally and directly from the root, grow into strong individuals who are confident of themselves even in the white world.

If young Indians were to follow the example of Vic's nephew who remained on his reservation until he reached maturity, they might be able to come to terms more easily with the demands of our time. This boy was steeped in the traditions of his people, and yet he was able to cope with the peculiarities of the modern world — I mean, what could be more twentieth century than IBM Data Processing! — whereas his friends, who had gone away to school, were preoccupied with looking backwards for their identity. By this I am sure we don't mean to imply that a job at IBM is necessarily the desired end result. The point is not IBM, but the fact that this young man achieved a certain success both within his own world and within the realities of our twentieth century civilization. Having achieved this, he is obviously in a better position to direct his creative energies from now on to problems outside of himself. He doesn't need to bog down in his own frustrations.

ALLEN QUETONE: In present-day society, our Indian way of life cannot be lived as it was in pre-Columbus times. Speaking from my own personal experience, the treadmill moves forward and if you want to keep up with it, you have to run with it. But in running, you neglect your children and their education.

I've looked at this from the standpoint of my own kids. What little is given to them is given by my wife at home, and only now and then by me because of the other demands on my time. Perhaps the first thing we should do is get off this treadmill and slow down a little bit and live as human beings ought to live. It may not be possible to do this all at once under the present circumstances, but we can at least begin. We can record the way life used to be lived by Indians, when every man had time for the essentials.

JOHN GARDNER: If you could bring life again into your traditions — in a new form that is true to the old but takes account of modern times — you could not only be sure of your Indian identity; you could also help the rest of us by bringing forward values that will benefit all people, Indian and non-Indian alike, and that the world so badly needs today. This, as I see it, is the challenge.

15

FIRST STEPS
TOWARD A SOLUTION

JOHN GARDNER: I should like to begin this portion of our discussions by doing something a little different. As you know, we have several younger people who have been sitting in on these discussions but who have not as yet actually participated. One of these is David Barten, who plans to make his career in education. I should like at this point to ask him to direct our attention to the future, so that we may explore what Indian education in the future should be.

DAVID BARTEN: I think it is significant that we have a mixture of older and younger people present at this conference. It is hard for us younger ones to look to the past. Certainly our task lies in the future; we have to work for the future. But if our work is to have a sound basis, we need the help of the older among you.

If you think back on the things that have been said thus far about traditional Indian education, they all had a very definite content. Discipline was a part of it, religion was a part of it, the family had a role in it. I would very much like to know what you think the Indian should be in the future, so that he can make his contribution not only to his own people but also to American society and the world. And, having established this picture, I would like to find out how we can take the content of this traditional education and give it a contemporary form, so that it honors the past, is suitable for the present, and at the same time fosters the kind of person you would like to see in the future.

HENRY OLD COYOTE: What should the Indian be in the future? As long as he knows his own background and knows something of the dominant society, the individual should be in a position to decide what he wants to be, whether he wants to be an Indian, whether he wants to be accepted in the dominant society, or whether he wants both. If he wants to be an Indian, he can still be accepted in the dominant society.

I have a cousin who can be Indian when he comes home and take a leading part in the ceremonies. He can come out of a ceremony and go to a neighbor and be just as much of a white man as he wants to be. He is the kind of person I have always admired. I have often wished I had his talents. He is accepted in both worlds. He can hobnob with the top brass in Washington, D.C. and still come back and be accepted by the humblest people on the reservation. That's how much territory he has covered by being himself. He is himself and at home in both worlds, and that's what I would look for in the Indian of the future. But each individual has to decide for himself.

In answer to your second question, "How can we bring this about?" It's up to the white man to decide. The white man can either keep that barrier up and force us Indians to put up that buckskin curtain, or he can let both curtains come down so that we can communicate, so that we can have a better understanding of each other. That is what I want: I want to be understood a little better. I am trying, but the white people are not trying to understand me. They are trying to tell me what they want me to do. They are trying to tell me what is good for me.

ALLEN QUETONE: I think we're finally getting around to the point that some of us were hoping we would eventually reach. The spirit, the feeling is here. For the benefit of those who may not know the Indian way, our communications with one another, even across tribal lines, are carried forth without any structured or firm lines of subject matter. The discussions, the council meetings, the visitations, will eventually reach that stage where the communication between individuals is such that there is a lot being said by words, and yet there is also a lot being said in the higher area of intuitive understanding, which words cannot express. I think we finally reached this stage at the Denver conference

The conference in session

on the third and fourth day. No guidance was needed. Questions were asked, discussions took place, people exchanged ideas; and this feeling, this spirit was there. In the Indian world, when you go to a powwow or when you go to any kind of meeting like a dance, if the spirit is not with the drum, it won't be a good dance. In other words, if there's bad feeling around that drum, or misunderstanding around that drum, even though you have a dance, it's not going to be right. Everybody can feel it.

What I am trying to say here is that we should continue with the subject that has been raised, but let's continue it in the Indian manner. It's a good subject. I'm sure all of us here have a great understanding of it; we have a great feeling about it, or at least know what we would like to see. I think the ideas and opinions that each of the persons around this table has will best be said in this atmosphere and climate of appreciation.

One of the things we decided before this conference began was that we would choose Indians to participate who have seen both sides and have come up with some ideas about what mixture of the non-Indian and the Indian world to use for themselves. The Indian participants' exposure to the two ways of life ranges from Max Hanley, who has probably been least affected by the dominant society, to Ernie Benedict, whose people are among those who have suffered most under the dominant society's impact. Non-Indians do not really understand the problems the individual Indian faces in reconciling both worlds. Every Indian who lives in the white man's world has to reconcile for himself exactly what he is going to take and what he isn't. The amount he takes depends on his own needs.

The real problem arises where we have two codes of behavior. I've noticed this in working with the Bureau of Indian Affairs, in sitting behind the desk at the Agency, where the Indians give me what I call the 'Agency treatment' until they get to know me. They will talk to me, but they won't really level with me. They're talking to the United States Government, and they have a very fixed attitude toward the Government. Only after they have some faith and confidence in their dealings with me will they really talk. Up until that time, there is a very definite conditioned behavior that Indian people have toward the white man and even toward other Indians if the latter happen to be in the Government. I think most of this conditioning has been built up over the years because in the past we've had nothing but non-Indian administrators; we're only just beginning to get Indian administrators. We want more Indians to be in positions to deal with other Indians in their affairs. This is the big push, I believe, for the present and near future. We want to be able to determine our future ourselves.

For the benefit of those who do not know, the current policy of the Federal Government and the Bureau of Indian Affairs is self-determination. The word from the top is, "Let the tribes make their contribution, let them exert their influence;" and the Government is offering Indian tribes a great opportunity to shape their future. Right now, some of the educators in the Washington office are trying to write up new proceedings and set up advisory committees that will give Indian tribes a chance to influence their local school boards. These are the mechanics Indian parents need in order to actually influence the way their child is educated, or to change what they feel is not good for their child.

HENRY OLD COYOTE: Along with that idea, my people are initiating a program of sensitivity training for new teachers who are coming into our area. Representatives of different groups, like the Cultural Committee and the parents, will sit down with these new teachers before the teachers step into the classroom and face the Indian children. The first session will be sometime before school starts this summer. It's a pilot project to see what can be done to give the teachers a little orientation.

In the Indian community as in any community, the teacher needs to know the customs and mores before he or she can do a good job. In relation to what we've been talking about, if teachers go onto a reservation, they should learn what goes on in that particular community in order to get · better results teaching.

ALLEN QUETONE: I am glad this is happening, but I am sure that many of our educators are very jealous of this much freedom or grassroots participation. The experts think they know exactly what is good for you, and they don't want their opinions to be disturbed. They are reluctant to permit any amount of participation by Indian people in the school system, and yet our public schools are supposed to be run by local people. As a matter of fact, one public school board with which I worked had no expertise in education and yet they ran that school. It was made up of the people who lived in that community — farmers, businessmen, and what have you. There is no difference to me between having these people run their school and having an Indian tribe run a school in its community, whatever the level of the tribe members and whatever their attitudes. It's exactly what happens in the rest of the country.

JIMMY BEGAY: Even now there are problems on the Navajo reservation about certified and non-certified teachers. We are using Indian teachers' aides. Some of the complaints from the teachers' aides to the school board go like this: "It seems as if I'm doing more than the regular teacher is." And they go on to show that the kids are turning more to them, since they are Indian, than to the regular teacher. There are a lot of teachers' aides who have the technique of teaching young people, but without a certificate or degree they are really nothing. And there are teachers who have certificates but are not able to teach anybody anything.

HENRY OLD COYOTE: Sitting here and thinking about this brings to mind the words of our last great chief, Chief Plenty Coups. When he was addressing his people, he recommended formal education for Indians. He said to the people: "Send your children to school. By going to school, you want to learn all you can about what the white man has to offer; but accept only the good things he has to offer. You can know about the others, but be able to tell the difference between them. By gaining formal education, you can be accepted by the white people. At the same time, retain your identity; try to keep the good things that your own people have to offer."

Now, a young man goes to school. He goes to secondary school, to high school and college. He gets his formal education; he works toward a degree. That's the white man's way; and when he comes out he sometimes forgets his Indianness, which he left at the door. He goes out into the world; he doesn't come back to the reservation. By the formal training he has had, he can make a better living away from that Indian reservation. You might say it's a brain drain away from the reservation. He could come back and teach his own people what he learned out there, but he doesn't do it.

An Indian who is well-versed in his own background but never went to school may be the best resource person we have. He has kept in contact with his own background. This other world of the dominant society that we are talking about in formal education is more or less alien to him. So while he may be the best resource person we can bring into the classroom to teach what we are talking about today, he's not eligible because he doesn't have a certificate. The teacher who is certified to teach, on the other hand, doesn't have the background. We need a person with a formal education, who has an inner understanding of the Indian and can project his feelings and ideas in the classroom.

ALLEN QUETONE: As I said earlier, the present policy of the Bureau of Indian Affairs is to allow input by the tribal councils and by the parents. But nothing happens. The Indians can't believe what they hear and don't know whether it's for real or not. Well, the thing to do is to take the position that it *is* for real, and act accordingly. Indian people are going to have to act and take the first step. This is their opportunity to move. Otherwise things may change again. As a member of Commissioner Bruce's staff at the policy level, I know that when a lot of these changes were being discussed for the first time, there was a lot of frustration in trying to implement them. The tribes didn't respond immediately and, of course, some Bureau field personnel openly opposed the new policy. We have an opportunity now to take a more active part in forming our school boards and in controlling our schools, and I think the idea is beginning to seep down to the field level.

JOHN GARDNER: As long as our schools are state schools, we are going to have problems. The government should not be involved in operating schools, whether they are BIA-run or simply ordinary public schools.

Let's suppose that we are talking about whether a particular teacher is a good teacher or not; whether a particular course sequence should be arranged one way or another. Who is qualified to decide? If a government agency decides, you won't win. What I mean to say is that it is not proper for the cultural and spiritual ingredients that make up education to be in the hands of civil servants and elected officials. Education should not be political football. You would never take a vote as to who a spiritual leader is. You would never do that kind of thing in an Indian tribe or in any one of your societies that has to do with the mysteries, or the deeper understanding, or the practical arts of life. These matters are not political; likewise, education is not political. The white man has yet to learn that when education is run by government, it loses its spirit. Freedom of choice for parents goes, freedom of conscience for the teacher goes, the full sense of responsibility is undermined in both parents and teachers — and the children suffer most of all. They lose in both enthusiasm and discipline. When education is not free, it can not be spirited. When students become dispirited, the nation's future is in jeopardy. I believe history shows, especially today, that these things are true as surely when the controlling government is democratic as when it is totalitarian.

If the Indian people could be allowed to pick somebody from among them in whom they had confidence, or let their wise ones pick him, and if they gave that person authority to run their education, then you would really be somewhere — especially if parents are given some choice between alternatives. This is the system in really independent schools, but it can hardly happen in public schools.

ALLEN QUETONE: There isn't an Indian who has reached maturity and been exposed to the schools and communities in which each of us finds himself, who would argue with you one whit, but we have been forced. So the next best thing we can do is to exert our influence where we can. We have to stand up and insist, "Okay, this is also a part of *our* government. This is a part of *our* school; therefore, we want to have *our* say in it."

JOHN GARDNER: You should do everything you are doing; but, if I may say so, you should also try to clarify the ideal. It is only when we can no longer reconcile the ideal with practical possibilities that we must of course compromise. The certification fight is a terrific fight, and it is one most white people at present still don't understand. It is a matter of mind control, culture control, the control of values, being in the hands of the state. The government is not intervening just against Indians; its certification requirements apply equally to white and black schools. Where certification is a legal power held by the state, many capable people are prevented from teaching, and teachers get in who ought not to be there at all.

I believe that what Henry Old Coyote said is true. Certain people who are qualified to teach certain subjects are qualified precisely by the fact that they are not in a position to get the ordinary certification. They have not been subjected to the kinds of things you have to learn to be certified. They have had other, more useful experiences. This is absolutely what qualifies them. But the fight goes beyond certification — it goes to the whole question of the control of schools.

Let me ask your opinion about what some educators consider to be the best hope. I wonder if you can see any possibility of setting up an Indian school somewhere in the United States that would be an independent school and not a government school? Because I have the feeling that if you could set a good example with one such school, it might be copied many times over.

As I believe you know, I am Faculty Chairman of the Waldorf School, an independent institution on the campus of Adelphi University in Garden City, New York. It runs from nursery through high school. If we see someone who we feel confident can teach a subject, even though this person has never seen the inside of a college, we can still hire him to be one of our main teachers. We have done it repeatedly, and there are half a dozen people in our school right now who are fine teachers, who have been with us for many years and carry important responsibility but do not have what it would take to get certified. That's how much freedom you still have in many places. In many of our states, educators can still run an independent school the way they please; but in order to do so, they have to scratch around and get the money. At our school, we stimulate the idealism of people to such an extent that they not only pay what it takes for their own children, but 95% of them also give money every year for scholarships for the children whose parents cannot pay. We are able to raise the necessary money because many people of all different income levels believe so strongly in us.

Perhaps you could organize a pilot school somewhere, run *by* Indians *for* Indians. I am convinced there is enough money around for you to get support without strings attached. Support with strings would not in the long run help. In an independent school of this kind, you could experiment and do things your way. You wouldn't have somebody telling you: these are the state-approved schedules, state-approved hours, state-approved curriculum, state-approved certification procedures; these are the approved textbooks. I admit that this would not be the cure-all for the Indian problem, but you have to start somewhere. You have to start in such a way that you will be sure of continuity and be able to change and grow as your own experience, not some political pressures, tells you to. I do believe a pilot project of this sort is the best hope for the future education of your children.

ERNEST BENEDICT: Last fall there was a showdown with the established educational system that was brought on by some Junior High School students. They had gotten so tired of seeing the Indians downgraded in the history books that when they came to that part of their history lesson, they objected very strongly. At first they went off and got some sort of authoritative help from other schools. Then they went back to the local schools and said, "What you have been teaching us is wrong, and we are not going to stand for it. We want someone to teach the other side."

The school officials wouldn't go along with them, so they dropped out. First they demonstrated. They stayed out of class, and they disrupted some classes, and eventually they were suspended. When the suspension was lifted, they wouldn't go back. Then a new school, called the 'Indian Way School,' was begun. It seems to be a free school from kindergarten to junior high school, and I think it is very experimental and uses volunteers, a number of whom are from the community and some of whom are white. Some of the white people may have teaching certificates, but the Indians do not.

ALLEN QUETONE: This must be related to movements like AIM that are underway in the United States, particularly in urban areas. AIM has started its own schools in Cleveland, Chicago, Milwaukee, and Minneapolis, where they simply bring Indian kids from all over town to one place. These schools have their own teachers and they're having some problems with the city school system because of certification. Even though the kids may not be getting the quality education they would be getting in the public school system, even though they may not have the buildings, the teachers and the equipment public schools normally have, they are getting more from the standpoint of being together, staying in school, wanting to learn; and they are getting proper attention. Apparently, everybody likes it. The Indian students like it, the parents like it, the AIM organization likes it. So it may be the beginning of a new movement in Indian education.

MAX HANLEY: The Indians are increasing very rapidly, especially the Navajos. So we're trying to get ahead and make enough schools for all these Navajos: hurry up before the water overflows the dam. We're trying to bring schools that are way off the reservation closer to the reservation, so that we won't have to haul these kids way off and spend so much money.

The Navajo Division of Education has people like me who go to conferences and different places and try to see what other schools are doing in neighboring cities like Albuquerque, Denver, Salt Lake City, Phoenix and Los Angeles. We are trying to get all the information and put it together. We hope it will give the Navajos a better idea of how to run their schools. This is our job. So I really am glad that Mr. Quetone invited me here. I don't know who told him about me, since I come from way down on the last part of my reservation. When I go back, I'll go to the different education chapters and report what you people are trying to do.

ALLEN QUETONE: The Navajos have come a long way. They have their own people who have conformed to the requirements and who are certified. They went and got a degree in teaching and served the time it took to be certified. They are educating the young people with Navajo philosophy but using modern techniques and methods. They're also cutting new ground themselves in terms of new methods of education as far as traditional ways are concerned.

JOHN GARDNER: Education is supposed to solve problems; it is supposed to bring up people so that they can find the solution to any problem. So it is very much to the point, even when we are talking about education, to leave education as such alone, and try to pinpoint the main problem. We have discussed the question of certification; we have discussed the possibility of an Indian-run school; and Max Hanley has just referred to the Navajo effort to bring schools back to the reservations. Are these the main difficulties you face, or are there more fundamental problems?

HENRY OLD COYOTE: I once heard a boy make a

remark that to me summarizes the essential problem: "The teacher is afraid of the principal; the principal is afraid of the superintendent; the superintendent is afraid of the school board; the school board is afraid of the parents; and the parents are afraid of the children."

So the problem, you might say, is how to get the children to go along with you. Students in various parts of the country are now asking to sit in on school board meetings to make their demands known. I believe this is healthy. They want to participate in planning. But here you will have to get the cooperation of the parents. Like me, I had my own ideas; but the older people knew what was good for me, what I should do and how I should conduct myself. I think parents must at least teach children to have some principles instead of turning them loose and letting them do what they please — giving them the family car, turning over the keys to them, and forgetting where they might go, like those parents I saw in Las Vegas.

I believe, therefore, that one solution to the problem rests with the parents and the manner in which they regard their child. They should take into consideration that it is *their* children whom the schools are trying to educate. If they have any love for their children at all, they should be receptive to them.

I believe we all need to communicate more with each other, with the child, with the parent, the teacher, the principal, the superintendent and the school board. We have to start somewhere. We can't take away all the television sets. But we can use some of the things children like, in order to get through to them and find out their likes and dislikes. And if parents substituted a little love and a little consideration for all the money, cars and television sets they give their children, if they listened to their needs instead of telling them to go off and not bother them, they might be surprised at the results.

I don't know. I wish I had the solutions. But I am thinking about it and looking for help just as you are. I have really enjoyed my visit here with you people, and I would say that I was very fortunate to be included in this conference. I have some good jokes and good stories and some positive thinking to go with me when I go home.

ERNEST BENEDICT: One of our earliest traditions deals with Captain Joseph Brandt, who was one of the first Indians who had advanced education in the white man's sense. He was supposed to have been very successful in either world; he knew his people, and he knew the white man very well, and he was able to cope with both. He was also able to express himself well, and some of his writings are really beautiful. He was a great man and highly respected. Apparently his children, who had the same advantages, didn't measure up, and he had to kill one of them in self-defense because of liquor.

The point I am trying to make is this. It takes an unusual, I would even say a superman, to be able to function in both societies. I myself have been pushed into both societies. I haven't had any say in the matter — and I find that I am not nearly as adequate for the job as our ancestor, Joseph Brandt, was. I would say that it is an almost losing battle for ordinary people. One solution is to give up and follow the white man's road, because they are so powerful. Some people have tried that; some have been able to get along pretty well as white people and have been pretty successful and happy. But most I have observed have not been able to make a go of it. As a result, there is a whole string of drunks on a Monday morning not only on the backroads of the St. Regis reservation, but also in the streets of Syracuse, Rochester and Buffalo. We're in a real predicament.

What is the solution? So far, the only thing that has been offered is heavier doses of the same medicine that caused all the trouble in the first place. I remember that I was forced to leave my family and go out to look for an education, for book learning. I was able to come back, but learning to live with my people again was a big job. It took me about 27 years to relearn the language so that I knew it well enough and could feel at home. My own family has scattered; my brothers and sisters are all over the United States. I am forced to obey the laws where my own children are concerned, and send them to school; so that they, too, are being pulled away from my household. I have very little choice in the matter; I am given very little freedom.

A boy selecting a career for himself is usually put under the guidance of teachers in the lower grades, and later under a professional counselor. Quite often it is they who determine the rest of that child's life. Recently there has been a tendency toward specializing at the high school level. At the age of approximately 14, a child is asked to make a big decision, whether or not he is ready for it, that will affect the rest of his life. It is a cruel thing. And if he is not up to it, it is the school counselor, not the parents, who makes it for him. The counselor decides that the child should take a vocational course that will train him for some kind of manual work or trade; or he decides that the child should take a course in the liberal arts so that he can go on to a university. So often the parents are neglected, and so often they are too shy to interfere. It is rare for parents to go and take a stand, because of their own inadequate background and education, and because of the ridicule that is made of them in the school system.

So I would plead for the return of children to their parents, so that parents can be the ones to influence the future of their young. The old traditional roles of uncles, aunts, grandmothers and grandfathers should be resumed and recognized as determining factors in the education of a child. If the present-day society won't give this to us, we will have to find some way to plead, to negotiate, and perhaps to drop out of the system and take back to ourselves the education of our children and the solidity of our family.

VICTOR SARRACINO: I don't think there is any overall answer at this time to the question of what Indians should be in the future, but if we could have similar conferences in the future, we could discover answers little by little. I would have to go home and consult with some of my people about what they feel is important for the individual, and what they wish to have taught in schools.

The real problem in educating Indian people today is the methods and techniques that are used. We have schools where there are new techniques of teaching, and where many things have been upgraded. But these new methods are so contrary to what we are used to that often our way and the new way don't work together. You can't follow one without neglecting the other. There are complaints from teachers who say, "You know, this child is not even motivated at home," because when the child gets home, he has things other than school work to do with his grandmother. Then when he has difficulties with the things he is supposed to learn at school, because they are so alien to him, the parents say, "The teachers aren't doing their job." What happens is that the child is left in a vacuum. He doesn't know who to listen to, because there is no coordination between the teacher and parent. I always feel there should be more workshops to get the teachers and parents together, as well as the principal, so that they can come up with some kind of system to work on this child. They need to join together to become child-centered, not catering to the child's whims, but finding the best way to reach him. Without that, they are just going against the stream, each trying to educate the child in his own way.

If you really want to get a child's attention at school, you have to talk about something in which he is really interested. The child's family may like to weave: find a way to relate what you're teaching to weaving, and the child will be impressed. The child may have just returned home from sheep camp and he's in school now: talk about something that has a relation to sheep, and you'll get that child's attention. This is the way I look at it, because this is the way my parents and elders used to talk to me. In fact, when I came back from the field, they would ask me, "How are the chili coming out? How about your watermelon, and your corn?" I would sit there and describe them, and I would learn from what I had observed.

ALLEN QUETONE: I have never had time to sit down with any of my kids' teachers or principals, but it seems to me that some of the things our schools miss are so obvious. For example, what makes kids react? What teaches them respect? What makes them listen and learn? I think what Vic just said is universally understood among Indian people —

everybody knows how a child has to be treated.

As I get older and look at kids now — look at my own children — I think the most important thing is the building of a person. Everything else will fall into place after that. I mean, what's so great about learning algebra? I have never used algebra since I've been out of school and it hasn't contributed to my well-being in any manner. It's fine to know; don't get me wrong. But the building of character should be given priority. The Indian way is to teach the child from birth to puberty about the importance of behavior and survival. Everything else will follow naturally after that.

VICTOR SARRACINO: That is approximately what I had in mind, but more of this kind of conferences and workshops need to be held to discuss and clarify these issues.

ARTHUR SUTTON: You fellows have a lot of bright ideas; you are smart men. But you are starting something here that is going to explode to the rest of the world. You're molding something like a snowball. You're going to roll it down to the flats and you're going to hurt some toes; you're going to hurt some feelings. But let's look at it this way. You're paving the way for my Indians to have a clear path to travel, where they will have better rights to get into the mainstream of life. Let's take it in this light. Give my Indians equal rights in schools; give my Indians equal rights in courts. That's all I have to say.

JOHN GARDNER: Many of those who are super-fired up over rights, as though these were more basic than anything else in a man's life, have this to say: "Men are all one. These racial and religious differences mean nothing. Men are the same as women, black is the same as white, red is the same as yellow, ancient is the same as modern: everything is the same." They have a concept of the universal human being that is good, but not good enough. It is by far too abstract. What is wrong with this idea of the universal human being, as put forward by merely legal-thinking people, is that it doesn't take any account at all of differences. That is good when it comes to equality before the law, but it is bad when it comes to creating, understanding, or reconciling cultures. If these people had their way, they would obliterate all real distinctions between cultures. As a result of their efforts to unite mankind, the Indian would simply lose his Indianness, his religion, his language, his customs. Humanity would end up as one homogenized, neutral, 'who cares?' unit.

Contrary to this concept is quite another idea, that has a better chance of bringing harmony among men, as far as their cultures are concerned. This idea is held nowadays by the relatively few whose eye is on the culture rather than the law. These people see that the abstract legal concept that erases distinctions between people, if carried too far, actually destroys culture and destroys individuals. Mankind is one whole, but it is nonetheless composed of distinct individuals. Individuals are very different from one another and want different things, yet if we wish each other well and will accept the rules of fair play, I can be educated fully in my culture and you in your culture, each can follow his different life-style, but we shall both of us work together harmoniously. We shall get along not because the law has homogenized us but because we are both children of the Great Spirit. This means that we share rationality and the desire to be good men. This kind of equality does not suppress the freedom to be different.

In this conference we have heard much concerning the rich traditions of the American Indian past. We have also heard how many of these traditions were suppressed and subsequently lost in an unwise effort to obliterate distinctions and remake the Indian in the image of the white man. In recent years, fortunately, there has been a growing recognition of the American Indian culture and a growing trend toward self-determination on the part of Indians. The sooner the Indians can get their separate footing again, and the freer they are left to develop their own new style of education, the more quickly we can take the next step together — reaching past the limits of our separate cultures, to see how your culture and our culture can join together for the common good. All mankind is in trouble today, and it will take the concerted effort of all — each contributing out of his freedom — to supply the remedy. It is with this thought in mind that I would like to conclude today's discussion.

16

IN PURSUIT
OF THE COMMON GOOD

JOHN GARDNER: There was a time when the white
man in America assumed that he alone knew what was in the
best interests of others. This attitude goes back to the early
missionaries, of whom we spoke at the beginning of these
discussions. But the ever-increasing problems we are encoun-
tering today confront us with the probability that the
majority way in the modern white world is not necessarily the
best way. There is no doubt among the white people present
in this room that the American Indian is the bearer of great
gifts from the past, which until now have been overlooked or
undervalued, but which have what it takes to bring health
back to our sick society. I would like for a moment to focus
upon the unique contribution the American Indian could
make to modern culture, just as he once provided the
groundwork for the American political system.

MARION GILLIAM: The other evening Henry Old
Coyote mentioned that one of the most important parts of an
Indian's education was the training to be a warrior, and that
in former times when a young man went out and fought and
won, he came back and shared his booty with his tribesmen.
Although wars of this kind have ceased to exist, he indicated
that there are still ways for Indians today to develop
generosity without the necessity of a battle beforehand.

Perhaps we could turn our attention to qualities such as generosity that were deliberately developed by the traditional Indian. In doing so, we may discover ways to bridge the culture gap and achieve a truly creative and responsive relationship between Indians and the dominant society.

HENRY OLD COYOTE: We Indians are taught to take into consideration the less fortunate members of our tribe. We believe that if you help a pauper who does not have means, you will get a reward, not from him but from some other source. There is someone listening, someone watching all the time; there is a great force looking down on you. So you will gain your reward from somewhere else. By having a soft place in your heart, by extending small kindnesses to people, you will receive their appreciation in return. They will extend their kind thoughts toward you. The more people you help, the more of those kind thoughts are extended toward you, thoughts that you may have another good day, or another year, or some more good seasons. Getting kind thoughts from people who express their wishes for your well-being means more than material things.

Our women are trained to do that. My wife, for example, might go down the street and see a man with both legs gone, holding a cup with some pencils. She will give him something, but she won't take the pencils. She would rather hear that man say "Thank you." As he says it, she might think, "This good thought is for my little granddaughter." The good feeling that man has for the gift she extended might be transmitted to her grandchild to help her grow up to be a young woman. The reason I always use that expression, 'a good day,' is that I try to express my thanks for the life that is given me; I try to show my appreciation in some small way for being allowed to enjoy this good life. It goes right back to some of our beliefs. The white man's world teaches us that we are supposed to economize, to save. To an Indian, to save is just like paying alimony; it's like buying oats for a dead horse.

That's a comparison of the Indian and the white man's way. It goes back to that number 'four' again. Where the white man says, "Faith, Hope and Charity," the Indian — the Plains

Indian, that is — says, "Love, Faith, Hope and Charity." So the things the Indian does are controlled by love, the love he has for his relatives or for his people, and by the faith he has in his beliefs, and by the hope he has for his people. And charity began during the old days of warfare when any war booty was shared with the people.

An Indian says that brothers and sisters are closer to each other than parents, because brothers and sisters have the same flesh and blood. They are therefore one people — not the same person, but the same people. So the love between brothers and sisters is expressed by the deeds they perform for each other or for each other's offspring. The reason my wife is keeping one of her grandnieces is to show her niece how much she loves her. Our grandniece started living with us when she was two weeks old. She's eight years old now and is still living with us. To show my love for my older sister, I adopted one of her boys, the oldest one. So although he is my nephew, he is also my son today. And in order to do it really right according to the white man's way, I legally adopted him through the State Court.

To show my faith, I grew up and performed certain services without complaint. That's why my wife gets after me. She says I don't know when to say 'No.' So I neglect my own duties because I want to be of service to my people, and I perform these services without complaining. I lose a lot of sleep. I lose a lot of meals. But I am willing to do things at my own expense for the betterment of my people. By doing things and performing services, I hope that my people may see a better life. If nothing else, I hope they will have pleasant memories and be satisfied. I am willing to share everything I have with my people. It doesn't matter if I am on the lowest pay scale — I still am willing to share with my people. I try to live by the preachings of the older people: that is, by Love, Faith, Hope and Charity.

The only thing people will remember you by when you leave this world is how you conducted yourself in life. Since you can't take your personal belongings with you, it makes no sense to hang onto your worldly possessions and hoard them. As they say, "Enjoy life, because you'll never get out of it alive!'"

ALLEN QUETONE: Generosity is probably one of the strongest feelings or values Indian people have. It is always there among our people. Many in the dominant culture, especially the local non-Indian communities, view this trait in Indian people with low regard. It conflicts with the acquisitive nature of the non-Indian cultures.

We are always willing to share. We have a pool, a source at home, and it's called 'traditionalism.' Within each of our tribes there are certain people who are traditionalists. These are the people who hold onto and perpetuate our customs and traditions. They provide those of us who are on the outside, who are in the Bureau of Indian Affairs and other places across the country, with an opportunity to come back and participate. In other words, any time I want to charge my battery, I can go back and enjoy many of these Indian ways: I can participate in them, I can regain a feeling for our traditional values; and I might say that it's the greatest feeling there is. On the Fourth of July, for instance, there will be many, many camps and visitations, and dancing and talking. You will see the things we have been talking about, such as generosity, practiced by people who do it as a matter of course, where it's no big thing, where it's just a way of life.

VICTOR SARRACINO: In times past, as we all know, the economy of the Indian people was based on the soil. In this day and age, the economy is based on wages. What happened is this. The Indian had a lot of land, but he didn't develop it. He meditated and prayed and went through his traditions because he didn't want to commercialize anything. But other individuals came along with other ideas. One commercialized lightning and made electricity. Another built a factory that was supposed to be good for people, and he polluted the air and the waters running into the lakes. And more and more people developed the land and built factories and sent out ships and polluted more lakes, more oceans, more air — while the Indian just sat there and continued to do his traditional thing. Now, one individual who had been building and polluting said to another, "Did you ever notice that there is an Indian standing on top of the Capitol Building in Washington, D.C.?" The other replied, "No, I never did; but I bet I know why. After you take all of the land away from the Indian, there is no other place to put him but on top of that building!"

Now people are suddenly beginning to realize what they have done to the waters and earth and air. They are trying to learn how to correct it and are turning to the study of ecology. Maybe the Indians will have a hand in it this time; maybe they can help. The little story that I told, I told facetiously, but I still think there is logic to it and it ties in with what was just said. This is our chance: this may be where we can make a real contribution.

The Indian people have always had a great respect for nature and would hesitate to tamper with her greater wisdom. For example, I don't know whether it's right to prolong life too far, when perhaps through natural circumstances we were supposed to have gone on ahead. I know an old man who lives in Laguna, and he once said to me, "When I was a young kid, I used to pray that I could live as long as I possibly could. Now the longer I live, the lonelier I am, and you're the only person who comes to visit me. I look forward to your visits, but if you weren't around, I'd be the loneliest man. I used to pray that I'd get old, but every morning when I try to get up, I ache in my knees. It's just a painful thing." He walks around, and he told me, "One day I fell down and I got up as fast as I could. I didn't want anybody to see that I fell. I advise you one thing," he said, "Don't pray too hard to live so long!" Medical science can be a great help to mankind, but it should be applied wisely.

ARTHUR SUTTON: The Indian lived next to nature. He studied nature; he wanted to find out what gave that tree life and where it came from. You, as a non-Indian, must come back to the earth and live next to nature in order to receive instructions about the origins and purpose of life.

The Indians know there is a Supreme Being. Where did they get this knowledge? By studying nature. Everything they learned, they learned through nature. The life we are living, the air we breathe — they studied all these things. They even went out to fast, that they might be able to know better.

They wanted to find out where everything comes from. Do we do this today? No. But we need to know these things in order to get a better understanding of what we are trying to accomplish. We can learn these things by living closer to nature.

JOHN GARDNER: It is so interesting that the white man's civilization has been studying nature for hundreds of years, and the more it studies, the less it learns. We have to be clear about the fact that it is not enough simply to live next to nature. It depends on *how* you live next to nature, *how* you study her. Here, too, the Indian can show the way. If it is only the brain and not the heart that is listening for nature's message, her deeper teachings will not be heard. Her mysteries will be stripped away by a cold manner of knowing. Her life will be first exploited, then destroyed in an arrogant and selfish way.

ERNEST BENEDICT: Most of the councils of the Iroquois people are open to all of the tribes. Children especially are encouraged to attend. When they do, they see all of the older people — parents and grandparents — humbling themselves and showing gratitude to the Creator. The councils always open with a prayer that is addressed to the people. This prayer asks them to show gratitude for the many things they are given to enjoy — things of earth, things above the earth such as the sun, the moon and the stars — and tells what these things bring to people and what their function is according to the intentions of the Creator. The children are then encouraged to take their turn in leading the prayers of thanksgiving. We believe there are seven of these thanksgivings per year, and sometimes nine, depending on what year it is. And the gratitude is always there in these thanksgivings. Our people see that the things of nature are given high priority, because the things of nature can exist without man but man cannot exist without nature. If white people harbored this spirit of gratitude for the gifts of nature, the earth would become a better place in which to live, because you do not destroy what you cherish and revere. Perhaps we Indians can help to bring this mood of thanksgiving into the dominant culture.

ALLEN QUETONE: The dominant society's attitude toward the Indian has changed a great deal in recent years. There was a time, as most of you have said, when the government used the educational process to Anglicize us, to remake us in the white man's image by forcing Indian kids to go to school, by forcing them to cut their hair, to speak English, and not to sing Indian songs. The missionaries said our traditions and rituals were evil. These were some of the extremes to which we were subjected as a people, and to a limited extent these attitudes still hold true. But in the main, I think this country of ours would like to do right by us now, if it knew how.

As far as I am concerned, the Myrin Institute is a prime example of how the white man is trying to help. By initiating this meeting, it has provided us with an opportunity to bring some of the beliefs, values, and teachings that we hold dear to the attention of other Americans. Most of us have found that the non-traditional upbringing of young Indians is not producing the best results, and that we might be well advised to adapt some of our traditional values to our present needs. Our hosts seem to feel that these older values could also be of help to non-Indians. We have just mentioned a few of the qualities that are specifically developed by Indians and form a part of the broader scheme of values that we respect and foster at the very outset of a child's life on this earth. So I hope these discussions will be published and made available to people who are interested in furthering a deeper under-standing of education and the good life.

JOHN GARDNER: The crucial question we face is whether or not it is possible for the Indian of the future to remain in close touch with his own traditions — his myths, rituals, arts and so on — and at the same time manage to cope with the main stream of civilization.

There are some people who believe that you can be religious in one part of your mind and technical-scientific in another part, and that these two parts go along side by side very nicely as long as they keep their distance — in other words, as long as you are able to live with a double mind. You could view the relationship between the traditional

American Indian and the modern white man in the same way. But, in fact, most people in our country do not even do that. Our present civilization has cut down the Indian culture; our way of thinking misunderstands the old Indian values, is suspicious of them, pushes them out. Even those who increasingly acknowledge the Indians' right to their culture tend to feel it can exist 'side by side' with the white culture. We agree to this, and yet we see that there is a certain conflict that cannot be ignored but must be solved. This is not a superficial conflict, nor is it basically a racial one. It is the conflict that starts when there are two ways of thinking, the intellectual and the intuitive, and when they are not equally valued as leading to truth.

As I have said before, these two ways *can* and should reinforce each other, but only when both are understood and believed in. Simply to claim that as an Indian you are going to take the twentieth century white man's culture into yourself and be half that, and at the same time remain half Indian, means that you are going to take the present unresolved and very real conflict between the white and red cultures — and between the intellectual and intuitive approaches to reality — internalize this conflict and find yourself at war with yourself. One part of you will then disbelieve and hold in contempt what is most precious to the other part of you!

As I see it, this question touches not only the heart of the Indian problem, but also the problem of modern twentieth-century life. In a certain sense, the dilemma in which the modern Indian finds himself is the very same dilemma that white civilization faces. All of us should realize that in the past there was great spirituality in the white man's culture, too. We have had great seers, great poets, artists and holy men, great heroes and men of prowess. But we white men have cut ourselves off from our spiritual heritage, and in the process, through the education we are forcing upon them, we are threatening the Indians with the same fate.

Our contemporary white education, which we pass along also to Indian children, has mainly to do with the external skills that supposedly enable you to get along in life. Such an education contains none of the inner mystery that exists in the sacred traditions you have been telling us about. But the mysteries of knowing and feeling and doing that once existed in the white man's culture can be found again, and in new ways. I believe it is important that not only white but also Indian children be made aware of these traditions in our culture. It will not do to have the spiritual lore all on the side of the Indian and only materialism on the white side. Indian education will not bring the red man together with his white brother until it includes awareness of the high spirituality that existed in the white culture of former times and seeks out examples in the present culture of where new spirituality is beginning to appear.

For instance, what are the Indian children in the first, second, third, fourth, fifth, sixth and seventh grades of their public school reading at the present time? What are they studying? If they studied what is truly great in white culture, they would feel sympathy and respect for it. But if our own sacred traditions and spiritual deeds are not taught in the state schools, how can a healthy Indian child — and, for that matter, a white child — help feeling contempt in his heart for white civilization?

ALLEN QUETONE: I don't quite understand. I just went back mentally to the late 1930's when I was in school, and I don't see how I could have been taught more respect for this country and white people than I was. I was a real piece of clay for my teachers, and I was given an ideal picture of what this country is about. But it was a myth. I learned about this country's history, about its geography. I also learned about its great men: George Washington, Abraham Lincoln, and so on. I had great admiration for these people and still do, but when you go out into the world and face the realities of life, there's no connection. In other words, I was in a situation to be ideally taught, but what I was taught had no connection with life.

JOHN GARDNER: But your teachers didn't quite do what I had in mind. The really deep traditions of the non-Indian cultures are not found primarily inside the confines of the United States and its political history. There is greatness here, too, but it cannot be compared to what made Indian culture great. To make the right comparison, you would have to go farther back. Teachers would have to show how the heroes, saints and seers of olden times, in Europe and Asia especially, developed themselves: how they thought and felt, what disciplines they underwent, what their experiences were. The more of all this an Indian child receives, the closer kinship he will feel to his white brothers. By the same token, the more aware a white child becomes of the great spirituality in his own past, the more readily he can comprehend the wisdom behind American Indian traditions.

If we wanted to find the original roots of white culture when it was still healthy, so to speak, we would have to go back in time: past the American Presidents and political leaders and past this country's battles and territories. I do not mean to say that there are not now great people in this country. There are and have been many. George Washington was a great man. Perhaps Lincoln was still greater. And very recently there was George Washington Carver, about whom I have just been reading. He was an almost contemporary scientist, a black man who discovered many uses for the peanut and the sweet potato, and did a tremendous amount to help his people. He got up at 4 o'clock every morning of his life and went into his laboratory, where he asked God, "What would you have me do today?" What he achieved was so remarkable that the joint Houses of Congress in Washington invited him to speak to them. So here is a great man, and if children were taught honestly about the genius of George Washington Carver, they would gain a tremendous respect for what black people can create and produce in modern times. The same would be true if they were taught about other great men in the history of our civilization, so long as their achievements were seen as the result of an inner path of development.

I admit that it is difficult to reconcile the differences between the noble ideals of great men of the past and all that is going on today. But it has to be done. You have to look beyond the present scene — not only backwards into the past but also forwards into the future. The spiritual greatness of the past lay in its religious grounding. The greatness of the present lies in its special materialistic kind of science. If the future is to be great at all, for any of us, it must combine science and religion into a new approach to reality. Educators must show how this is to be done. Our concern at this conference has been primarily for education, and we hope to have taken a step towards the kind of education that will nourish and strengthen Indians and non-Indians alike, and that will turn to positive *advantage* many differences between our cultures that too often in the past have caused misunderstanding and antagonism.

I have said several times that I do not think it is appropriate to talk much during this particular conference about future, specific methods of education. In the end, however, everything will depend upon the finding of such new methods. If you will forgive the personal reference, therefore, as we close our conference, it may be of interest to characterize briefly what we are trying to do at Adelphi University in the Waldorf School (an elementary and high school) and in the Waldorf Institute, a graduate school for teachers. I have been surprised to discover how the education children at our school receive parallels at every stage and level, in a fully modern way, what you have described of your wise traditions. I am encouraged by the confirmation you give to what we have been striving to do.

For example, when we take in children at kindergarten and primary levels, the spiritual nourishment, the motivation and discipline we try to give them, comes through exactly the same kind of stories that you have been telling us. It comes through legends, myths, fairy tales, and fables. We do not bring children up on those homogenized readers that are so commonplace in schools today; we use real legends, real myths, real fairy tales — from Egypt and Greece, from central and northern Europe, from the American Indians — through the fifth grade at least. These myths and legends play a part in everything that goes on. We can use this material because we do not think of it as amusing or beguiling or escapist, but as seriously true. It is not the modern *form* of truth — but truth is one under all its forms. This older form of truth is, we believe, the best preparation for those who want to make use of truth in its modern form without being captured by it.

Our basic concept of how to educate a child holds that the child is educated first in his limbs, through his actions and deeds. His bodily development at this stage is shaped through imitation. Imitation is the basic method of learning in the pre-school years. From the ages of approximately 7 to 14, we believe that you have to speak to the child's heart — always to his heart. It makes no difference what subject you are talking about: you have to relate it to his feelings. The subject has to unfold through joy and pain, through laughter and sorrow, not primarily through abstract concepts. A child who is taught in this manner will develop a strong and active emotional life; he will develop depth of feeling. As this same child approaches the high school years, he will gradually develop an enthusiasm and capacity for thinking in its modern abstract form. He will begin to formulate his thoughts independently. So: in his earliest years, the child learns through imitation; then he learns through feeling, through respect for authority; then at last he comes to his independent judgment. At the end of a sequence that *begins* very close to what you have described as the Indian way, our students find themselves fully equipped to handle college studies of every kind. They start as doers and as artists; they end with a good percentage of Phi Beta Kappas and Ph.D's.

We try to take every subject — whether it is spelling, history, physics, math, or grammar — and do with it what Henry Old Coyote did with the tipi, what Victor Sarracino did with the pueblo. We try to teach in such a manner that every fact and idea is what it plainly is, but so that it also has overtones and undertones, has other dimensions that are connected with the mystery of life. We try to do this not in a preachy, but in a pictorial, dramatic, story-like way: in fact, in just the way you have been presenting things here. We want a truly religious feeling to permeate everything — religious not in the church sense, but in the sense that recognizes the divine in all existence, just as the Indian has always felt it.

A further observation that has to do with what the

Indian past can contribute to the future of education may be in order. The modern child in a suburb or city tends to be nervous and depressed. One reason for this, in our opinion, is that he cannot work enough with his hands as Indian children used to do with clay and cornstalks. Much greater emphasis has therefore to be placed on the arts and crafts. This applies to high school, and even college, as much as it does to early childhood. As some of you have said, it is the excellence of every detail in an art or craft, and the thought behind it, that count. Children must be taught in such a way that they set to work with that same real seriousness with which Mrs. Old Coyote does her bead work, even if they do not achieve such beautiful results. For example, if as an artist you wish to portray trees, you must surely first, as a student, have developed a feeling not merely for the trees but for the clouds above and for the directions around, for life itself, and for the seasons: in other words, for all of those elements that surround or play a part in shaping trees. If education has first awakened in you a sense for the creative mystery of these things, and then you take up some material — whether it is music, the dance, paint or clay — this creative power will work through your hands and feet to shape the material in a more wonderful way than if this sense were asleep or dead.

VICTOR SARRACINO: Does your school include a college, too?

JOHN GARDNER: No. It goes only through the twelfth grade. But we offer postgraduate training under the Waldorf Institute of Adelphi University. The Institute trains teachers in new methods of education, and Adelphi awards a Master's Degree in education upon the trainees' completion of this one-year, full-time program. We admit a very small group to this program — only 20 students each year.

We should love to see two, three, or four Indians in it. We know that a teacher trained in the Waldorf Institute can be as different as night from day from most of the people you get with the ordinary training in education. If you could send us one or more of your people from time to time, we are sure that when they returned you would find them wonderfully in tune with what is Indian and at the same time

able to achieve success in the mainstream of twentieth-century life.

With your forbearance, I should like to add one other comment concerning the extraordinary importance for the future of both the red man and the white of a right relation being established between practical work and education. Everywhere in the white man's schools a main purpose of education today is to teach you so that you don't have to work! Presumably, the better educated you are, the less work you will have to do. You can then get other people to work for you; and if not other people, at least machinery. But a sounder attitude would be something like this: If I am going to shake my friend's hand, I don't want some machine to do it for me, even if such a one could be invented. In other words, a man should not want to be saved from all the 'work' in this world, because with the right attitude he can find in almost all of it both joy and satisfaction.

In connection with the important question of work, we can see that one of the sad paradoxes of modern progress is that the time- and labor-saving techniques of which we are so proud make it almost impossible for us to be *still* enough to know our own mind, and thoughtful and caring enough to conduct the proper ceremonies of life. Though we are supposed to have acquired all these means and tools in order to enjoy greater ease and leisure, the net result is that we don't have enough time to call our soul our own. And we hardly have the strength to move from here to there. What is more, we don't at all receive the inner fulfillment that comes from work done in a skillful, artistic and sacred manner.

Youngsters today don't have enough of an opportunity to work, to lay their hands upon the earth and transform it. I am convinced that if we look to the not distant future, our industrial civilization will have proved that it is too expensive for the earth. You don't have to be a prophet to see this; you just need to be a little observant and apply common sense. By industrializing further and further, we will reach a breaking point where everything will begin to go wrong: with nature and with people themselves. We have already reached this point. It must be emphasized, then, that only by preparing all young people in all schools to use their hands, to be much closer to nature, and to find joy and satisfaction in useful work, can we help modern times to take a turn voluntarily for the better, before it is too late.

VICTOR SARRACINO: I have a question. You have spoken of two ways of knowing. One is religious and the other scientific. Could an individual be scientifically religious; in other words, both in one? Earlier, you seemed to suggest this.

JOHN GARDNER: I don't know how much you want to go into this question. There are people who would give this an easy answer. They might say, "There is no conflict at all between the religious way of knowing and the scientific way, because religion tells you that God made the world and science tells you *how* He made it. So where is the conflict?" But this to me would not be a proper answer, because our present form of science often gives explanations of how things are made that push the divine creative spirit out completely. If everything I do is explained in terms of material substances and forces, and all my choices, all my actions, all my affections are simply the inevitable working out of these forces, and I am told, "That's how God runs the world," I feel that someone is trying to kid me. My religious idealism will then amount to no more than superstition.

If one were to be scientifically religious, and religiously scientific, it would involve a radical step forward for both modern science and traditional religion. This is precisely the step I feel must be taken — soon, and especially through education. It seems obvious that the future of the world will depend primarily upon how science moves, because science is in control today. All technology and industry come out of science; the practice of all doctors and, ultimately, of all farmers, preachers, and teachers comes out of it also. Thus, the character of our science determines the character of our civilization.

If science is such that it gives us sound, practical explanations and at the same time reveals ever more and more the presence of mysterious powers and of a higher wisdom and love in all things, we will, as Henry says, 'have a happy day.' And we will be scientific and religious at the same time, to answer Victor . . . But we must accept the fact that probing intuitively to the deeper secrets of existence demands that we *first* make the effort to be better people — because real wisdom requires real goodness. If mankind were to emphasize those qualities that we have discussed in this conference: respect, generosity, discipline, courage, purity, to recall a few, we would take an upward turn. If not, our downsliding will bring us to disaster.

MARION GILLIAM: I think the greatest challenge for mankind today is to develop an awareness of the Divine around us and within us, and to tap this creative source in solving the problems that confront us. If you look at the really great scientists — not super-technicians but truly creative individuals — they have all been deeply religious men, though usually in unconventional ways. Take the example of George Washington Carver mentioned earlier. When he went into his workshop to try to find uses for the peanut, he left all of his science books outside. He went in and said to the peanut, "I know that you have secrets to tell me, things that I can use to help my fellowman." He concentrated on the peanut and it gave him the inspiration for things he could produce to help his people. From the things I have heard at this conference, I should think that, in many areas, the Indian comes close to this type of thinking.

VICTOR SARRACINO: This is the reason why I am not at liberty to discuss many things that actually are the very basis of what you have just mentioned. The Indians do have a certain way of communicating with nature, but they don't want to commercialize any of these things. Some of the Indians here may go one step further than others in their explanations, because we don't all have equal restrictions at the same level.

MARION GILLIAM: That point is clear. We have not wanted anybody to speak of things that could be misunderstood. I simply wanted to say that I have been impressed by how much more open to inspiration from nature the traditional Indian was and is than I am! I do hope that the white culture can learn from the Indian how to observe

what is around us and how to understand what all forms of
life have to teach us.

HENRY OLD COYOTE: When most white men hear
that an Indian receives messages from various sources, they
expect an animal or bird or plant to have written a memo to
him telling him what he should do. But that's not the way it
is. An Indian believes there is a message in everything you see.
If a person is able to interpret that message, then he is
communicating. That's what we mean when we say we have
ways of communicating with nature, we have ways of
interpreting nature. An animal or bird doesn't actually have to
talk to me, but it carries a message if I know how to look for
it.

You just spoke about a man talking to a peanut. If
people saw him doing that, they would probably think he was
crazy. That's why we hold ourselves in reserve when we get
into things like this. We are afraid that these things will be
distorted and misunderstood and that the poor Indian will be
made to look ridiculous. You might call it being secretive, but
if you believe in these things yourself, and if you are sincere,
you will find the secrets out for yourself. We believe that no
person has the right to ask another what he says when he
addresses himself to the Supreme Being. I don't even have the
right to ask my wife how she addresses Him when she
meditates. This is what we mean by secrets.

JOHN GARDNER: A good comparison of the 'secret'
with the 'scientific' way of looking at the world can be found
in medicine. Apparently it was not the Indian custom to cut
into people. Although the illness might be anywhere inside of
you, the medicine man didn't open you up. By contrast,
modern medicine is based very heavily on incisions and
dissections. And these customs aren't limited to human
beings; animals of all kinds are also cut into. American
medicine is getting to the point where ten animals are said to
be dying in experiments every second, allegedly in the service
and for the benefit of mankind. And as Henry mentioned
earlier, even children are forced to kill countless animals in
biology classes — in their case, to learn things that are already
well known. So when you talk about whether or not science

and religion can come together, it depends on what science you have in mind. The purpose of the Indian's secret science, or way of knowing, was to keep whole things whole, because only when they are whole is the living presence, the soul or spirit, really there. When you start cutting into things unnecessarily, it's another matter: the mysterious presence withdraws. Your findings are plain, but they are only of the body. The treatment that results is addressed only to the body.

VICTOR SARRACINO: That is why I said that any time anybody wants to build a house, he has to get permission from the proper individuals to cut into the ground. There is a man who lives by our village. One time he actually stood at the edge of an enormous hole that had been bulldozed out of the earth and cried. It was just like cutting into the body when they cut into his Mother Nature. He knew that the earth had a lot of value and that uranium would be extracted from it which could possibly be used for the good of mankind. But it was extracted in a destructive way, all the same.

JOHN GARDNER: Our conference has come to its end, but I should like at this final moment to voice the feeling I think we have all had about what made traditional Indian methods of educating so great. It is this that our present methods lack. This is where reform in the white culture must begin. I am going back to all that each of you has had to say about respect and reverence.

As a teacher, I feel that American education today, in its approach to all things great and small, lacks reverence — respect for life. And the future of education must lie in an attempt to convey knowledge and skills in a new way, an artistic and religious way, so that every detail awakens reverence, awakens respect. The man who is so inspiring for all Waldorf schools and for our Myrin Institute for Adult Education, is Rudolf Steiner, an Austrian educator who lived at the beginning of this century. Steiner was also a scientist and a man of vision. He said that reverence is to the soul what food is to the body. It is the ground of all true feelings; it is the beginning of wisdom; it is also the beginning of power. Reverence is a breathing out of the person toward the All Life, the Great Mystery. And the power that returns to the person from his reverence is grace, a grace that makes his life creative. These are the two sides of the 'magic' to which we referred earlier. It is through reverence that we learn to know the depth and fulness of life, so that the multiplication of trivial knowledge is quieted down and given direction. And it is through reverence that the 'magic dream' and the 'magic power' that are lacking today can be renewed. Thus happiness really lives in the out-breathing of reverence and the in-breathing of grace. I believe this is what each of you has said during this conference. The American Indian has helped us to understand these things, and there can be no doubt that he and his traditions can inspire a better education for all American children.

APPENDIX:
WHO'S WHO
AT THE CONFERENCE

JIMMY BEGAY is a Navajo who accompanied Max Hanley to the conference. He has taught the Navajo language in the Navajo Community College and helped develop a program for literate and non-literate Navajos. Most recently, he has been evaluating Navajo schools for the Navajo Division of Education. Jimmy received his education at Fort Sill Indian School, at Haskell, the University of Kansas and Grand Canyon College in Phoenix. He is 39 years old.

ERNEST BENEDICT is a Mohawk from the St. Regis Reservation, half of which is in the United States and half in Canada. Ernest was born on the United States side. While working as an electrician in a factory in New York State, he read a story about a young Ojibwa boy who came out of the backwoods and was forced to go to a government-sponsored school. This boy so disliked school that he ran away to return to his family, but was found frozen to death before he reached home. The incident drastically affected Ernest's life. He left his job and became founder and head of the North American Indian Traveling College. He felt that if it was such a traumatic experience for many Indian children to be taken out of isolated communities to go to school, it would be more humane to bring the school to the Indians in their communities. This is what he is trying to accomplish through the Traveling College. Ernest is also Professor of Introductory Indian Studies at Trent University, Peterboro, Ontario, and Educational Officer on the Canadian side of the St. Regis Reservation: He is 56 years old, is married and has four children.

MAX HANLEY is a Navajo who was a BIA employee for 33 years, until his retirement in 1962. Max is 74 years old and lives in Tuba City, Arizona. He is currently working for the Navajo Division of Education evaluating Navajo schools in the western portion of the reservation. Two and a half years prior to this, he worked as a field representative for the Navajo Culture Project, and traveled through the western portion of his reservation collecting information from the old, traditional people, which was then transcribed in Navajo for eventual use in Navajo textbooks. Max received his education at Shiprock Boarding School, the Sherman Institute at Riverside, California, and the Albuquerque Indian School. Max is married and has 12 children, seven grandchildren and three great-grandchildren.

HENRY OLD COYOTE is a member of the Crow tribe, and was born and lives in St. Xavier, Montana. Henry became interested in the lore of his people a number of years ago and started compiling information on them back in the 1950's. At present, he is Coordinator of Indian Studies at Hardin High School in Montana, is a member of the Central Education Commission of the Crow Tribe, and an advisor on bi-lingual programs. In addition, he helps in the actual teaching of children and is involved in adult education programs in six school districts. Henry is the spokesman for his tribe in all dealings with the government. He is also a member of the Crow Cultural Committee, is coordinator of various programs on the Crow Reservation, and is the official Master of Ceremonies for the Crow Fair and for all Crow dances and gatherings. Henry received his education at the Big Horn Country School, at the Phoenix Indian School in Arizona and Rocky Mountain College in Billings, Montana. Henry is 60 years old.

STELLA OLD COYOTE is Henry's wife and accompanied him to the conference. She is a member and Treasurer of the Crow Social Activities Committee for the Big Horn District in Montana. Stella is one of the few remaining full-blooded Crow Indians. She and Henry have two daughters, one son and one grandchild.

ALLEN C. QUETONE, Chairman of the conference, is a great-grandson of Chief Stumbling Bear, famous Kiowa chief and signer of the Medicine Lodge Treaty of 1867, which created the Kiowa, Commanche and Apache Reservations. He graduated from Fort Sill Indian School, enlisted in the U.S. Air Force and in 1947, helped organize the American Indian Veterans Association. He is a graduate of Oklahoma City University and has served as moderator and consultant on panels at the University of Oklahoma and the University of New Mexico. He was two years on the staff of the Commissioner of Indian Affairs in Washington, D.C., and is now Superintendent of the Concho Agency, Concho, Oklahoma.

VICTOR SARRACINO is a member of the Laguna Pueblo Tribe, which is located approximately 40 miles west of Albuquerque, New Mexico. He was the recipient of a Ford Foundation fellowship for leadership training and was selected to be the first Tribal Judge of the Laguna Pueblo. He has held an elective position in his Tribal Council for 18 years and is now Executive Secretary of his tribe and its official interpreter. He is also a member of the All-Indian Pueblo Council, representing 19 tribes in New Mexico, and is Program Director for higher education. Victor is on leave of absence from the BIA, where he worked in the Office of Tribal Operations, in order to obtain his B.A. Victor, who is 44, is married and the father of six children.

ARTHUR SUTTON is one of 14 Arapaho Chiefs and is Tribal Councilman. He is also Deputy Sheriff for Blaine County, Oklahoma, and Vice Chairman on the School Advisory Board at Concho Indian Boarding School. He is Chairman of four Mennonite Churches and Assistant Pastor of his local Church. In addition, he is a Board Member of the

Indian organization of Alcoholics Anonymous. Arthur is 66 years old; he is married and has 11 children, 22 grandchildren and one great-grandchild.

* * *

SYLVESTER M. MOREY, Chairman of the Myrin Institute, is a former New York advertising executive who retired in 1968 from the Chairmanship of the Board of Geyer, Morey, Ballard, Inc. He is currently a member of the Visiting Committee on the Native American Program at Dartmouth College.

JOHN F. GARDNER, President of the Myrin Institute, has been a teacher and school administrator for 25 years. He is Faculty Chairman of the Waldorf School, Adelphi University, Garden City, New York; Director of Adelphi University's Waldorf Institute for Liberal Education; and Adjunct Professor of Education at Adelphi.

MARION G.H. GILLIAM, Vice President of the Myrin Institute, is also Secretary of the J. Henry Schroder Banking Corporation and a Trustee of Adelphi University.

DAVID A. BARTEN is succeeding John Gardner as Faculty Chairman of the Waldorf School and is completing, at New York University, his Ph.D in the history of higher education.

OLIVIA L. GILLIAM has been Executive Secretary of the Myrin Institute for the past three years.